EVERYDAY

Real-Life Buddhist Teachings
& Practices for Real Change

* * *

Awareness * Acceptance * Appreciation * Action

Wendy Shinyo Haylett

Everyday Buddhism

Everyday Buddhism: Real-Life Buddhist Teachings
& Practices for Real Change

Cover designed by Wendy Shinyo Haylett

Visit the Everyday Buddhism website at:
www.everyday-buddhism.com

Printed in the United States of America
First Printing: November 2019
Cabin Publishing
Fairport, NY USA

ISBN-978-1-7341638-0-3

TABLE OF CONTENTS

TESTIMONIALS OF REAL CHANGE
FROM REAL PEOPLE

"I'm pretty sure you just changed my life. You said that your suffering can be a Buddha. I have been struggling and I can see how I can use this pain as a teacher, as a Buddha."—MP

"I've been so inspired by your podcast. I've struggled with the teachings in the past. The sentence structure of ancient texts is like trying to make sense of Shakespeare! Thank you for making these powerful tools accessible." —GF

"I wanted to tell you how thankful I am for your podcast. You have helped me to find peace within myself by studying the Dharma through your podcasts, as well as through other literary resources inspired by your teachings." —DR

"Podcast related theory and praxis so well. Effective, inspiring, empathetic." —SE

"I am beyond appreciative to have found your podcast! Your podcast feels like having a conversation with someone I can learn so much from. I needed this in my life and you've already helped bring a calm to the chaos I was feeling earlier today! —S

"Wendy makes Buddhist concepts relevant to the daily practice of life. She serves as a catalyst for personal growth and fulfillment. Thanks, Wendy for your insight and wisdom!" —MM

"Sometimes when hip hop music and celebrity gossip turns into racket, I turn to Wendy's podcast. She's very humble and great at explaining terms and theories. Listening to a podcast a day keeps my mind interacting with those around me." —KF

"Love this. Super relatable content. I like the emphasis on how these concepts are hard, which is why we need to practice them. It feels helpful without being judgmental." —F

"Thank you for taking time to share your knowledge with such practical language and easy to follow explanations. I've been studying Buddhism on and off for years, and your lessons are right up there with some of the best (i.e. Pema). :)" —RA

"Wendy and Everyday Buddhism are a welcome addition to the plethora of podcast choices. Her teachings are smart and simple and relevant and real." —BBM

"I just wanted to say that having only recently discovered your podcast, your knowledge and your application of practical buddhism has brought me a lot of peace and an incredible amount clarity. Thank from the bottom of my heart." —TR

DEDICATIONS

This book is dedicated to my precious teachers, from Gautama Buddha through the teachers who taught me in person or through books, from all schools: Theravada, Mahayana, and Vajrayana.

May their aspirations for all beings to be free from suffering and have the causes for happiness be realized. May everyone be content and well, every day and everywhere!

I would like to acknowledge Frank and Gretchen Howard, my first in-person mentors; my first refuge Lama, Drupon Sonam Jorphel Rinpoche; and many other teachers (past and present) who have influenced me including H.E. Garchen Rinpoche, Khenpo Sherab Ozer, Thich Nhat Hanh, Taitetso Uno, Nobuo Haneda, David Brazier, Gregg Krech, John Tarrant, Stephen Batchelor, Clark Strand, Gary Snyder, Dōgen, Shunryu Suzuki, Je Tsonghkapa, Master Shantideva, Shinran, Manshi Kiyozawa, and Shūichi Maida.

A special bow of devotion to my Sensei, Rev. Koyo Kubose; his late father Rev. Gyomay Kubose; Adrienne Kubose Sensei; Rev. Albert Bloom and Haya Akegarasu; my Bright Dawn family of Senseis and lay ministry students; and the teacher and Buddha always at my side, my wife, Renée Seiyo Phillips.

SETTING THE TONE

"Discarding all elements of supernaturalism and magical thinking, one returns to the mystery and tragedy of the everyday sublime. Instead of nirvana being located in a transcendent realm beyond the human condition, it would be restored to its rightful place at the heart of what it means each moment to be fully human. Rather than devoutly repeating what has been said many times before, you risk expressing your understanding in your own stammering voice."

Secular Buddhism: Imagining the Dharma in an Uncertain World
— Stephen Batchelor

USING THE PRACTICE & REFLECTIONS SECTIONS

At the end of each chapter there are two sections, a practice and a reflection. Action means putting what you're learning into practice. Try doing the practices suggested at the end of each chapter to make the Dharma your own in your everyday life.

Reflection or meditation is part of that action. One teaching on how to be a student of the Dharma is to "hear, think, and meditate" on the teachings. This means going beyond just reading and to immersing yourself into the teachings. This immersion needs to go beyond mere words and concepts.

The reflection section is to help you pause and immerse yourself into a poem that can take you beyond rigid concepts and into the "suchness" of what the words in the preceding chapter were trying to express. It is through poetry that I have been able to express things exactly as they are. It is only in poetry that I can speak to you without the concepts words create—stopping time, ending the separation between us, and uniting us in the immersion of suchness.

Yes, words are needed to write poetry, but the form of these words come from suchness itself, come from all life through me to you. As Shunryu Suzuki said "when you do something, you should burn yourself completely, like a good bonfire, leaving no trace of yourself."

PREFACE

IN THIS BOOK AND THE PODCAST THAT SHARES ITS TITLE, my goal is to talk to everyday people about Buddhism in an everyday way—the way I wished people talked to me when I initially began studying it. There were some Buddhist teachers who wrote books and taught classes using concepts that a Western or American mind could easily grasp—and who minimized the use of complex terminology or Sanskrit and Pali words—but only a few.

I realize there were far more of those teachers in the 1990s when I started my search and study in earnest than in the 1950s, 1960s, and 1970s when the true pioneers of American Buddhism found their places as our teachers. And for that I am grateful. But it still took a hefty dose of dedication and persistence to make enough sense of the teachings to apply them in your everyday life.

To me, it seemed like trying to learn calculus when all I thought I needed was to do the math required to balance my bank account or create a simple business spreadsheet. Yet, in hindsight, the calculus (or big-picture understanding of continuous change) is necessary to effectively apply the simple math Buddhism offers to everyday life. And it isn't as complicated as it looks when you find a gentle guide to walk you deep into it. My stubborn personality and desire to learn made me a tenacious student willing to take that walk deep into the lists, cosmology, philosophy, and theology to get to the psychological core that makes Buddhism an invaluable practice for happiness.

And as I continued to learn, practice, and eventually become a Buddhist teacher and lay minister, I realized that despite a person's interest in Buddhism they were unlikely to apply the same time and effort required to make enough sense of the teachings to use in their lives—especially in the Internet age where the virtue of patience is declining in reverse correspondence to the quickness and availability of information.

I remember sitting and talking with the directors of the Tibetan Buddhist center I belonged to, one evening after a class I taught in Buddhism Basics. I distinctly remember saying these words, "I would love to be a part of a Buddhist center or sangha that focused on Buddhism without the complexities of cultural rituals or the focus on guru devotion. Maybe I need to start one." They both looked at me, with what I subtly detected as gentle eye-rolls or winks and said, "good luck."

The center directors, Frank and Gretchen Howard, devoted much of their adult lives to establishing Mahayana Buddha Dharma in America and built a thriving Buddhist center. The foundation of everything I learned of Buddhism came from those initial years of study and practice with Frank, Gretchen, the sangha, and the visiting Tibetan teachers. I had accumulated tons of knowledge and information over the years I threw myself into study and practice, but looking inside, I clearly saw that none of it was mine yet.

As Stephen Batchelor wrote in the quote at the beginning of the book, "Rather than devoutly repeating what has been said many times before, you risk expressing your understanding in your own stammering voice." That was the risk I wanted to take. Through my association with The Bright Dawn Center of Oneness Buddhism, I was learning through practice that to make the teachings of the Buddha my own, I needed to bring them into everyday life and not silo them off in special secret practices from special teachers, at special times in special places. If there is one thing I'd like to emphasize in this book, it is this: When you make any teachers more special than what is in your life at this very moment—things as they are—you are moving farther away from true understanding and aligning yourself with the delusion that spirituality is "out there" or something other than life as it is.

From the beginning, Bright Dawn turned my thinking around: From a Buddhism "out there" possessed by special enlightened masters who I could only hope to hang around with long enough so that some of their enlightened mystery would rub off on me, to a Buddhism tried on and conversed with in the "mystery and tragedy of the everyday sublime." Like Batchelor, my aim is to help myself and others awaken to nirvana in "its rightful place at the heart of what it means each moment to be fully human."

INTRODUCTION: SEIZE THE MIND

"To cover all the earth with sheets of leather—
Where could such amounts of skin be found?
But with the leather soles of just my shoes
It is as though I cover all the earth!"

And this the outer course of things
I myself cannot restrain.
But let me just restrain my mind,
And what is left to be restrained?"

— Shantideva, Chapter 5 - Vigilant Introspection
from "The Way of The Bodhisattva"

THE FIRST THING YOU SHOULD KNOW ABOUT BUDDHISM is that it is—above all—practical. For those of us in the West, it can be considered more a blend of philosophy and psychology than a religion—and can be practiced despite your religious affiliation. The laboratory for the study of the philosophy/psychology is 100% accessible and portable because it is essentially a study of the nature of our own minds, with the practical goal of living a life that allows the mind to be peaceful and healthy.

The next thing to remember is that Buddhism is an experiential path. Although you may understand what you hear or read, unless you apply the teachings to your life, the results won't be realized. And, as the Buddha said, don't take it on his words, you need to try the methods in your own life to see if they work for you. If they do, accept them; if not, reject them.

Associated with the experiential concept is the fact that there may be some things you can't understand or accept. That's fine, but don't reject them because you can't understand them immediately. Investigate. Check them out by observing your own life. As one of my teachers said, "put them on a shelf and pull them out later to try them on again." Or as another of my teachers, Frank Howard said: "look for the Dharma in your life and you will become the Dharma."

As a Bright Dawn lay minister, I was trained from the beginning to write what is referred to as "Dharma Glimpses" or short Dharma talks. This has conditioned me to turn my mind toward the Dharma throughout the day to discover glimpses of teachings in my everyday life, which I then share with others.

My goal in this book is to share my experience of bringing Buddhist teachings inside with a mission inspired by Rev. Gyomay Kubose. In his words:

> *This Buddhism can be explained in simple, everyday language and practiced in every aspect of our daily life. Yet, it is a unique Buddhist life-way, non-dichotomized and non-dualistic, that will bring about a peaceful, meaningful, creative life, both individually and collectively.*

Be An Insider

Would you like to make every day better? This book is for you. It's not just for Buddhists or those exploring Buddhism. It's for everyone: All of us dealing with situations beyond our control ... things that stress us ... people that make us angry or hurt ... major life transitions ... overwhelming circumstances ... fears and self-doubts ... anxiety ... depression ... and being stuck in the past or telling ourselves stories repeatedly. Or just the small, everyday annoyances like rush-hour traffic, noisy kids, bosses who don't listen, and cars that won't start.

These are the things that make our days dissatisfactory—or even downright miserable—sometimes. But what does that have to do with Buddhism? Isn't Buddhism a religion? Yes and no. That's the fun (or exasperating) thing about Buddhism. There are very few, if any, answers. It's mostly about learning to be in the questions.

If you know anything about or even heard a little bit about Buddhism, you may have heard that Buddhism is about suffering. I call that the bad news of Buddhism. Suffering is a downer word, of course. And you might not categorize the problems I just wrote about as suffering but they cause you unease, right? Unease is suffering. It's not the suffering of pain, death, or poverty. It's the suffering of every day, the sort of problems that arise at work, or in our family life, or in our daily commutes, or at the grocery store. Buddhism is essentially about how *not* to get dragged down by the unease found in every day—big or small.

And here is the kicker: We think the things that cause us trouble in life—the things that "make us" angry, stressed, fearful, resentful, and on and on—are "doing it to get us." Maybe we don't think that exactly or make that direct link, like that long line at the store on a day when you are already late for work is a situation created for the sole purpose of causing you stress. You wouldn't admit that is how you think, would you? Of course not. Neither would I. But guess what? That's exactly how we act every day.

That's how our minds and our bodies are programmed to react. We are hard-wired to react that way. The amygdala, a part of the limbic system in our brains, controls multiple functions including processing memories, decision-making, and emotional responses (including fear, anxiety, and aggression). One of the things that happens to us when we are presented with a conditioned, unpleasant stimulus in our environment is that the amygdala produces an unpleasant or fearful response. And, as the stimuli continues to happen, we are conditioned to see these things as threats.

All of this is happening inside us. Yet our perception is that something out there is a threat. The Buddha knew nothing about the amygdala as a researcher or neuroscientist, but he observed himself in his environment and awoke to the fact that suffering can only be relieved by our thoughts and behavior, not by adjusting the people and things in our world or appealing to an all-powerful God. He firmly embraced and taught that the "buck stops with me."

Everything is about perspective. Everything in our lives is about how we look at the things that happen to us and in us, and how we behave accordingly. Nobody can force us to see things another way. We need to own our own perspective. We can't blame it on anything or anyone else.

What the Buddha Discovered is Also Within You

Remember when you were a child and first realized that people get sick, get old, and die? Remember asking why? Remember wondering what is the meaning of life? Remember your determination to find out who you were and why you were ... and your determination to use your life to make a difference; to make your life meaningful? What happened?

Speaking for myself, I got caught in the pervasive habit that is life: working, taking care of family, continually trying to get more comfortable—more comfortable jobs, more comfortable homes, food, and clothes, in the pursuit of pleasure. Hidden away in our homes, watching TV, going to the movies, the mall, on vacation, in the search for more and more comfort, more pleasure—yet held captive by those pleasures.

And, as the story goes, that is exactly how the Buddha lived, too. Even though he lived 2500 years ago in India, his life was very much like a relatively comfortable middle-class life many of us live today. Siddhartha, the historical Buddha of our time, or Buddha Shakyamuni, was born into a ruling family and was kept protected, comfortably locked inside the palace gates away from the aged, the decrepit, the poor, and the sick.

One day he convinced an attendant to take him outside of the gates and eventually went out four different times, each time seeing a sight he hadn't seen before. On the first three trips, he saw an old person, a sick person, and a corpse. The attendant told him that each of those conditions will happen to everyone, which, of course, made Buddha question the pervasive suffering. Then he went out a fourth time, where he saw a beggar with a sublime countenance—a wandering religious person who had given up his comfort to devote himself to finding the end of suffering in his life.

Siddhartha was like those of us who have searched—or are still searching—different religions, philosophies, and spiritual practices. Like us, he was confused and anxious by a life that is guaranteed to be touched by sickness, old age, and death, and was looking for something to make it better. He first glimpsed the promise of peace in the serene face of the religious wanderer, beginning a spiritual shopping trip—very much like we may have experienced—going to different teachings, trying different and sometimes extreme practices. It is written that the Buddha went so far as to eat only one grain of rice per day, being able to feel his spine through his stomach—until he realized that starving wasn't the answer—and that the answer was more likely found in the mind than the body.

He began to contemplate—to meditate—eventually awakening to a perspective of life as an inside job. And, at the urging of some of his fellow seekers, he began to teach and did so for 45 years, until his death. He taught many different people and modified his teachings to fit his audience. Yet each contained practical insights and tools to help them understand the difficulties and dissatisfaction of life.

His teachings spread from India and were interpreted differently as they were adopted by different cultures, eventually becoming different philosophical schools. From India to Ceylon, Thailand, China, Korea, Japan, and Tibet—with Tibet having the most extensive collection of the teachings. When China invaded Tibet and thousands fled to India in the late 1950s, the teachings then spread to the West, for which we are very fortunate.

Despite an incredible variation of schools of thought and practice traditions emphasizing different aspects of the teachings, they all have the same goal: enlightenment, or as the

Buddha said, "the single savor of liberation, of release, of freedom...." This freedom, he taught, is gained by watching and mastering your thoughts, which are the cause of your actions and speech that ultimately lead to either pleasant or unpleasant results manifesting in your life.

The Tibetan word for Buddhist is Nangpa or "insider." It is only in our looking inside that we will discover answers to any of our questions or solutions to any of our problems. It is what the Buddha set out to do when he left his palace. The Buddha sought what I believe we all have sought in our individual life's journeys. Who are we? What are we doing here? Why are things the way they are? It is a crazy-making question that can either haunt or enlighten.

One of my favorite lines in the television sitcom, *Everybody Loves Raymond*, is delivered by Robert, Raymond's TV brother, during an episode focusing on the same big question Raymond's daughter was asking: "Why did God put us here?" Robert, in mental torment, looks to the sky and says: "You mean God made us smart enough to ask the question, but not smart enough to know the answer?!!"

I think most of us, living in the illusion that we aren't smart enough to know the answer, quit asking the question. And, out of frustration with this inability to understand our lives—let alone control them—we carry on trying to influence, change, or control our external worlds.

In the West particularly, there seems to be little or no reinforcement—from our peers or from that external representation of the world in the media—to seek an internal understanding or solution to any of our discontent, unhappiness or suffering. No one seems to believe that they possess self-awareness, wisdom, and the capacity to change their lives or the lives of those around them.

In an early Buddhist scholarly book, the *Abhidharmakosa*, or *The Treasure House of Knowledge*, Master Vasubandhu wrote these words in 350 A.D., more than 1650 years ago:

Deeds cause the multitude of worlds.
They're movement of the mind and what it brings.
Mental movement is a deed of thought;
What it causes, deeds of body and speech.

The *Dhammapada*, sayings commonly attributed to the Buddha from his teachings, expresses the same theme:

Preceded by perception are mental states,
For them is perception supreme,
From perception have they sprung.
If, with perception polluted, one speaks or acts,
Thence suffering follows
As a wheel to the ox's foot.

Preceded by perception are mental states,
For them is perception supreme.
From perception have they sprung.
If, with tranquil perception, one speaks or acts,
Thence ease follows
As a shadow that never departs.

So, where do we find that liberation, that release, that freedom? In our own minds. It is our minds that will free us. Think about this for a second the next time you're tempted to say, "so-and-so makes me mad!" Can she really make you angry? Where did the anger come from? From your own mind, wasn't it?

A simple illustration of the brilliance of the common sense of the Dharma can be found again in the words of Shantideva in Chapter 6 – "Patience" in *The Way of The Bodhisattva*:

Thus, when enemies or friends
Are seen to act improperly,
Remain serene and call to mind
That everything arises from conditions.
[Verse 33]

And if their faults are fleeting and contingent,
If living beings are by nature mild,
It's likewise senseless to resent them—
As well be angry at the sky when it is full of smoke!
[Verse 40]

Although it is their sticks that hurt me,
I am angry at the ones who wield them, striking me.
But they in turn are driven and impelled by their hatred;
Therefore with their hatred I should take offence.
[Verse 41]

Of course, I, too, am capable of being possessed by that anger. Should I guard myself against the person who "makes" me mad or, instead, guard myself against my own thoughts that cause anger to arise based on mere shimmering perceptions? I am the only one that can get in my mind and heart, manipulating it to make me angry! Indeed, it is our own mind that causes us to be mad, sad, or peaceful, happy, and content.

And you can rest in knowing that is true based on these infallible teachings but check it for yourself in your own life. It was the Buddha who gave us the means, the tools to do that—to check it through his teachings, the Dharma.

Buddhism is full of lists. In addition to the Four Noble Truths and The Eightfold Path, there are the Ten Non-Virtues (or Freedom Vows), the Six Paramitas (or perfections), and on and on. I will share some of these lists with you later in the book and summarize them in Part 5: The List of Lists.

When I first began to seriously study Buddhism, I was overwhelmed by the number of lists (actually, I still am) and never thought I'd be able to remember any of it. But, as I began to incorporate them into my contemplation and daily living, it became easy for me to appreciate their practical value. They are all there as directions or guideposts helping us to answer the question, "how do we live to be happy?"

I will be using the Four Noble Truths as the backbone for this book, but I've repurposed them in a way that makes sense for you to use in your daily life. I'm not throwing away the traditional teachings that the Buddha awakened to, but I am repackaging them so that they are easier for us to use in our daily lives. I also hesitate to refer to them as either "Noble" or as "Truths" because both "noble" and "truth" are words loaded with connotations that position them as edicts on high, in the sense of ultimate truths one must believe, as part of a religious canon, or doctrines you must accept.

Buddhist teachings can help you be happy and help others to be happy, too. I'm avoiding language that emphasizes what you must believe, but instead what you should try to practice and see if it helps. From the writings that come down to us in Buddhist sutras, the Buddha didn't seem interested in these "truths." He refused to answer the sticky metaphysical questions like are we eternal or is there a God. Instead of having philosophical and metaphysical arguments, he stuck to the here and now and offered suggestions that helped deal with the dissatisfaction and suffering inherent in our human lives. Rather than having truth proclaimed and delivered to us, the Buddha taught that it was more important for each of us to deal with these issues in our own minds. Then we will be believers.

Even though I'm hesitant to use the term "Noble Truths" I will continue to refer to the four main points of the Buddha's teaching as the "Noble Truths" because that is how you will find them referred to when you explore them more deeply in your own research and reading. Another reason to use the word "noble" is that the origin of the word "noble" derives from the Greek *gno* (as in gnosis) meaning "wisdom" or "inner illumination" and the Latin meaning of "to get to know or to find out." It comes back to you getting to know or finding your inner wisdom, your Buddha Nature.

I offer another way of looking at the word "noble", as a courageous and authentic response to your life as it is, and the word "truth" as something YOU have made true for your life by practice and experience.

The Four Noble Truths as traditionally expressed:

1. **The unenlightened life is "suffering."** That life is suffering is the "bad news of Buddhism." Yet, a better translation of the "dukkha" or suffering is "difficult" or "unsatisfactory."

2. **The cause of this suffering is craving, or attachment or grasping.** When you like something, you want to grab it, possess it, keep it forever. This stems from ignorance about the nature of reality—the nature of what it is that really makes you happy.

3. **The cessation of dukkha is possible,** and the end is liberation or the realization of nirvana or enlightenment (bliss and inner freedom).

4. **The path or way to the end of suffering is explained through the teaching of the Eightfold Path,** which is the practice to achieve happiness for yourself and others—and, eventually, enlightenment.

The first two of the truths are sometimes referred to as "to be known" and the second two to as "to be experienced or realized." It's experience and realization that make these four points truths for you. They cannot be truths based on someone else's word alone. You need to experience or realize them yourself. And how I propose you do that through practical concepts you can put into practice.

To help us look at the Four Noble Truths in an everyday way, I've reframed them while still adhering to the essence of what the Buddha taught. I certainly don't believe I can improve on the Buddha's teaching, but in following the Buddha's approach of customizing teachings to the concerns and situations of the audience, I've rephrased the Four Noble Truths.

The Four Noble Truths in an Everyday-Buddhism way:

1. **Awareness: Life is crappy sometimes and we suffer.** This is the Awareness and understanding we need to get familiar with and know to be the truth of our human existence. Awareness prevents fear and confusion. **Awareness** is the first principle of the Buddha's teaching because it is necessary to first be aware of how things really are before we can begin to accept, appreciate, and act in the ways we must act to minimize our own and others' suffering.

2. **Acceptance: We suffer not necessarily because life is crappy.** I'm sure we've all had the experience of being relatively content EVEN when we are in a crappy phase of life. We don't suffer because of the circumstance in our lives but because we grasp or cling to things being something other than they are. We grasp at things we want and don't have; we grasp at getting rid of the stuff we don't want. The way to ease or eliminate that suffering is to learn to adopt an attitude of active **Acceptance**. As my Sensei and his father, Gyomay Kubose, taught: "Acceptance IS transcendence."

3. **Appreciation: There is a way out.** The way out offers a path of sincere appreciation for the teachings of the Buddha and the new awareness and acceptance that we now have for life as it is. This is the **Appreciation** phase. When we stop focusing on things we want but don't have or pushing away things we have but don't want, the things that are right in front of us take on a new shine. We truly begin to experience life. We appreciate everything in our life.

4. **Action: The way out is practicing the Eightfold Path. This is the Action Path.** When we are aware of things as they are and we begin to accept and appreciate life as we experience it, the right actions become more obvious and sensible to us. "Right" actions are the way the actions of The Eightfold Path are phrased, as the right actions to take. Yet we need to chill a bit around the rightness of right. These are not commandments or moral directives but suggestions about what actions may be the most effective. When studying and practicing the Eightfold Path, relaxing your grip on the necessity or "rightness" of having to do certain things exactly the way you interpret this "rightness" will be beneficial for you. Think of the word "right" in this respect

as the suggestions your trainer, Yoga teacher, piano teacher, or golf pro might give you to help your practice.

Circling back to our adolescent wish to make life meaningful, we see that Buddhism can be a refuge and roadmap for transforming ourselves so that all our activity becomes meaningful activity. We don't look for meaningful activity to transform us, but through our own transformation, life is meaningful.

Our mind, when properly prepared, becomes fertile soil for the bloom of compassion and wisdom—a fruit benefitting both ourselves and all other beings. We must become the peace we seek.

PART ONE:

AWARENESS · WISDOM

–1–

RIGHT VIEW: RIGHT UNDERSTANDING

Oneness Formula – by Rev. Koyo Kubose
$U = 2I + 2A = E$
U = Right Understanding
2I's = Impermanence and Interdependence
2A's = Acceptance and Appreciation
E = Enlightened Living

I BELIEVE I BEGAN GROWING INTO A BUDDHIST FROM A VERY YOUNG AGE, beginning with childhood night-time visits from someone I described as a wizard who presented stacks of books and said he came to teach me wisdom.

This continued through a life-long fascination with watching the way my mind worked. I have been examining my mind ever since I can remember, trying to understand how I was thinking ... what I was thinking ... why I was thinking ... and who was doing the thinking.

Socrates struck a kindred chord to the great Buddhist masters and teachers when he declared that "the unexamined life is not worth living." And it was 40+ years of that examination that brought me to complete confidence in the Dharma and its capability for creating happiness—not just for me, but for everyone. My mission for the rest of my years is to share the teachings and methods with as wide an audience as possible.

If you ask people what they think of Buddhism they typically respond with words like peaceful, calm, and enlightenment. Yet, when they begin to get to know Buddhism through reading or going to a Buddhist center or temple, they experience things they don't understand or that confuse them and it either starts them on a search for another type of Buddhism or they re-create Buddhism in the image of other religions by putting their hopes and expectations for that peace, calm, and enlightenment on something or someone outside of themselves like gurus. The harder work of examining their own thoughts and behavior is either avoided, or overlooked, or never presented to them as an integral part of the path.

I often have people ask me, "What is enlightenment?" And, as I grew into Buddhist practice and worldview, I have asked other teachers the same question or I asked them the taboo question, "Are YOU enlightened?" My view on enlightenment has changed over the years, evolving from a state I am trying to attain that is not of this world to a clearer view of what is in front of me right now. I now explain enlightenment as shining a light on things as they are, as something that comes and goes as you open and relax your awareness, allowing things as they are to be visible exactly as they are.

Enlightenment is about using wisdom and compassion to open your eyes to—and stay aligned with—the correct view, then continually harnessing that view to overcome the deluded thinking that causes you to say and do the wrong things in a confused and ignorant effort to be happy. It is a replacement of wrong thoughts and actions with right thoughts and actions until you are no longer planting any more bad seeds. Soon your soil will be fertile and beautiful, containing all good seeds that will produce only good fruit.

I think many people feel their lives can't be changed, or they have no power to change, or that their lives haven't really begun yet, or they are waiting for the right conditions, or their lives are already over. How do you feel about your life? Is it motivated by a big story—something bigger than yourself and your own ego-driven perceived wants and needs (which are the results of an attachment to seeing illusory life as real)? Or is it motivated by an authentic being-in-the-world?

The Buddha offered his followers an opportunity to become part of a big story. It is a story of how afflictions are met with a noble (courageous and authentic) response. It is a story of how our own internal energies, which sometimes feel so destructive, can be transformed into a power that can create happiness and remove suffering in ourselves and all other beings.

How can we accomplish that transformation? Through our own mind. It is our own mind that causes us to be mad, sad, peaceful, happy, and content. It is our mind that will free us. You can rest in knowing that this is true based on these infallible teachings, but you need to check it for yourself in your own life. It was the Buddha who gave us the means, the tools to do that—to check it by applying his teachings, the Dharma, in your own life.

Basic Buddhist Teachings

Before I introduce more about Right View so that you can apply it in your life, I will give a very abbreviated glimpse of the types of Buddhist teachings and practices that are commonly followed across the world. The teachings of the Buddha, or the Dharma, have essentially evolved into three main traditions:

The Theravada, or Tradition of the Elders

The Theravada tradition is the oldest school, dating to the time of the Buddha. It is the path of individual liberation and is predominantly practiced in Southeast Asia. The core emphasis of this tradition is on renunciation, discipline, and simplicity for the cultivation of virtue, contentment, and loving-kindness. Its focus is to escape the constant circle of suffering and reach individual liberation through monastic discipline.

The Mahayana

The Mahayana arose after the Theravada and is the path of universal—rather than individual—liberation. The Mahayana laid the groundwork for a Dharma practiced not just by monks, but by laypeople who could integrate practices and principles into everyday life, using wisdom and compassion, the two wings of enlightenment. It first became familiar in the West in the form of Zen Buddhism. The core approach is the Bodhisattva vow, the wish for universal liberation—or the altruistic intention—emphasizing helping others while awakening ourselves through a practice of love, compassion, and wisdom.

The Vajrayana

The Vajrayana vehicle emerged later among Indian and Himalayan spiritual practitioners and yogis. It is sometimes referred to as the "Diamond" or "Lightning" vehicle due to the use of tantric practices that are thought to enable the possibility of attaining enlightenment in a single lifetime—in contrast to the many or hundreds of lifetimes it is thought to take using Theravada or Mahayana practices. It is like a rocket path that uses intense energies like rocket fuel. These practices can be skillfully utilized or mistakenly applied, calling for the need of a teacher or guru. This vehicle also incorporates both the Theravada practices of discipline and ethics and the Mahayana view and practices of compassion and wisdom. It is predominantly associated with Tibetan Buddhism and its emphasis is on the use of skillful means to realize your inner nature.

From these vehicles, too, arose many schools and subdivisions of teachings and practices that are beyond the scope of this book. Despite the divisions and traditions, the "Three Trainings", the "Four Noble Truths", and the "Eightfold Path" are teachings common to all. The "Three Trainings" are Ethical Self Discipline, Meditation and Mindfulness, Wisdom and Love (or compassion training).

The Four Truths and all the Buddha's teachings are based on common-sense. I think many people, Buddhists and non-Buddhists alike, would accept the basic premises applied in the Four Truths: If you know and accept that there is a problem, you need to first find out what caused the problem before you can try to fix it. Otherwise, you might spend a lot of time doing the wrong activities, wasting time and money trying to fix the problem, based on a faulty understanding of its cause. In business, this is referred to as root cause analysis.

On a personal rather than universal level, the first practice is to look at what might cause your own particular unsatisfactory-ness, uncomfortable-ness, or pain. It's funny. From my observations of people, I think many people don't even look at what their own discomfort is made of or where it comes from. They bury or repress their own personal suffering and the suffering of those around them, or they accept it as a lousy, natural condition that can't be changed because life IS indeed "shit and then you die." I'm talking from my own experience, too. I am not immune.

Looking further, let's examine what this suffering or dissatisfactory stuff is made of. I know it seems like a ridiculous exercise in pessimism, but not only does Buddhism focus on this suffering or 'dissatisfactoriness' but it classifies and categorizes the types of suffering.

The Buddha taught that there are three basic types of suffering:

- **The suffering of suffering.** This is the obvious suffering—what most people equate with suffering—actual physical or emotional pain. Illness, injury, loss, grief or even disappointment.

- **The suffering of change.** This is the fact that your body, mind, and all the people and circumstances of your life constantly change and deteriorate. This is what one of my teachers used to summarize as, "attached to every pleasant experience is a lousy end." Whether it's the last of the cookies, or the death of a pet or family member, or the loss of a job, it's all made of the stuff that will change, decline, or disappear.

- **The suffering of conditioned existence, or pervasive suffering.** This is the suffering that results from having a condition, or nature, that is impermanent and changeable, based on the conditions that bring our bodies, minds, all phenomena, and all circumstances into existence. It is this conditioned existence that causes the process of aging and dying, which begins at the moment of conception. It's the nature of our existence.

But there is a silver lining to conditioned existence and it leads to the Fourth Noble Truth. Since everything comes from the conditions that bring it into existence, everything: being, phenomena, action, or experience is a result of its causes.

Do you see the silver lining yet? It is this: change the conditions; change the outcome. If the causes change, the result will change. Remember I said, "Attached to every pleasant experience is a lousy end." Conditioned existence also guarantees that attached to every lousy end is the beginning of a new experience. Aren't you glad you stuck with me this far?

The Eightfold Path = The Way Out

This brings us to the Fourth Noble Truth: The "way out" or path to the end of suffering, which is the Noble Eightfold Path. The Eightfold Path can be grouped into three categories: wisdom, ethics, and meditation, which are the "Three Trainings" I mentioned earlier. But it is wisdom that is the main support of the rest. Without wisdom, the structure crumbles.

Although I said the Eightfold Path is a step-by-step process, it really isn't a path, as in "first I do this and then I can move to the next step." It is not a linear list, but a circle: a holistic system designed for the strength of all the components together. This circle structure is probably best understood by thinking of the Wheel of Dharma, or *Dharmachakra*. The *Dharmachakra*, the wheel of transformation, is used by all Buddhist traditions as a symbol of the path presented by the Buddha.

The Dharma Wheel is comprised of a hub, rim, and, generally, eight spokes. The hub is a symbolic representation of moral discipline or ethics, which provides the support needed to stabilize the mind. It's easy to understand how morality is necessary before a stable meditation practice can be established or a stable life can be enjoyed. If you are lying, stealing, or cheating on your spouse, your mind would be in a constant state of agitation, making it difficult to have a mindful life or establish the proper ground for a meditation practice to grow.

The rim represents mindfulness, enabled by moral discipline that, in turn, contains and holds together the eight spokes, or Eightfold Path of practice. So, again, you see the structure of the three categories of wisdom, ethics, and meditation I mentioned earlier. By applying this structure to your life, as a unified whole, you can transform yourself from someone who has trouble unsticking their mind from troubling issues (suffering) to someone who is able to remain calm and clear, despite the circumstances of life.

The eight spokes of the wheel are:

1. Right View

2. Right Intention

3. Right Speech

4. Right Action

5. Right Livelihood

6. Right Effort

7. Right Mindfulness

8. Right Concentration

The first two are grouped under the wisdom category, the next three under ethics, and the last three as meditation. Contemplating these eight practices you can see that without the first—Right View—the rest would be difficult to accomplish. How can you possibly know what right intention, right action, or right effort is if you don't have the correct view to begin with? Right view yields right intention, right thoughts, and action. Yet, they each support the others, like spokes on a wheel.

Right View = Right Understanding

Let's focus on Right View. It is a vast and continually unfolding concept for me. From the most basic perspective, Right View is a clear understanding of the Four Truths. If we have a clear understanding of the Four Truths, then we also have a clear understanding of the way things really are. We see things as they are, without the filter of expectations, hopes, or fears. The ability to see things as they truly, absolutely are means we have wisdom—which is not necessarily intelligence. In our culture today, wisdom is not something valued, but intelligence is, so this means turning some common, accepted thinking on its head.

David Brazier in *The Feeling Buddha* says that the Buddha would say "all views are wrong views." And I would agree. It is a warning on how dangerous opinions can be. If I am attached to an opinion, then it will inevitably get in the way of a clear perception of both subjective and objective phenomena. A good example is when a friend tells you something about someone you haven't met yet. Sort of like a warning about them, based on your friend's judgment of that other person. Your friend will say, "Watch out, she talks a lot!" Then when you meet that person, you may be hesitant to open up and be too friendly in case she talks your ear off. But if you approach the new person with an open mind, refusing to accept your friend's judgment, you may find out you love the person's conversation style and content and you hit it off!

We all know how dangerous views and opinions can be. Cooperation between people breaks down over them. People come to blows over them. Getting upset and taking what people say to us personally causes unnecessary suffering and clouds the mind. As David Brazier continues to say, "it is a case of a fire being caught by the ego wind."

Right view avoids both relativism at one extreme and dogmatism at the other. If we approach life with an open mind, we will experience the Four Truths, not just read about them as dogma. We will experience the suffering in the world, in all its manifestations. Right view enables us to see clearly and feel deeply, but we must be alert because we are playing with the fire of ego—our own and others'.

Brazier explains that just as when we purposefully create a fire, we bring together the fuel and a spark, while making sure the fire pit is sheltered from the ego wind, to be safe. "The inflammable material within us must be managed correctly. The spark is provided by our openness to the suffering of the world." Perceiving suffering within us and around us, causes the "spark that lights the fire of our spirit."

The suffering in the world is not something to solve on our own. We need to solve it together. And we can only do that by responding to our own and others' suffering with right view, the view that doesn't seek escape or a disguise of the existential reality of our lives. Brazier says, "When we have the courage to live life as it is, no longer running away...then we experience a profound relaxation in our heart. We put down the burden and no longer have to live defensively."

Right view is wisdom. Wisdom is renunciation. I imagine you're scratching your head now. Renunciation? You mean renouncing the world and becoming a monk? Nope. It's more than that. It's better than that, and it's easier than that! And it's something we all can do!

Renunciation in Tibetan means "authentic becoming." It does not necessarily mean living in isolation from the world, but a renouncing of the delusions that keep one from becoming one's authentic self. It means giving up clinging to the appearance of things as something or someone out there happening to you. It means that instead of grasping tightly to the things that will only cause us suffering, clinging desperately to things as we would like them to be, we surrender to things exactly as they are.

What do "things exactly as they are" look like? They look a lot like it is described in the *Prajnaparamita* (meaning perfect wisdom) *Sutra*. In the sutra, which is central to the teachings of Mahayana Buddhism, you will find the beautifully written wisdom of the "Eight Similes:"

> *Regard this fleeting world like this:*
> *Like stars fading and vanishing at dawn,*
> *like bubbles on a fast-moving stream,*
> *like morning dewdrops evaporating in blades of grass,*
> *like a candle flickering in a strong wind,*
> *echos, mirages, and phantoms, hallucinations,*
> *and like a dream.*

If we could really see life as it is, it would look like that. Life is not as real, solid, permanent, and unchanging as we think it is. Life isn't any of those things: solid, permanent, nor unchanging. Nor are we. Yet we are conditioned to see ourselves, others, and everything in life that way. At some level we all know our lives won't go on forever; our loved ones won't be with us forever; we won't always get along perfectly with our partners, friends, and families; we won't always have days full of sunshine and meals we love. Yet we behave as if all that is true—or should be true—and are continuously disappointed when it doesn't work out that way.

And we get up every day with the same expectations. These expectations are attachments. They are the root attachments of all other attachments. They are what create our "conditioned existence" and what block our right view. To have right view is to cling to nothing that you associate with as yourself and your life. If you cling to nothing there is nothing that you can't deal with. If you cling to a star, a bubble, or a dewdrop, you will be disappointed.

That is the absolute truth of reality. In Buddhism, we refer to the Two Truths: absolute truth and relative truth. Relative truth is the belief that we can hold on to a bubble and keep it for ourselves like we try to hold on to our youthful appearance, our reputation, our money, our family. The absolute truth is that we cannot hold on tight enough to keep it forever, because conditioned existence rips it from our hand. Yet we continue to try, in some desperate, neurotic belief that if we try hard enough, believe hard enough, it will make it so. That is how we generally live. That is the nature of conditioned existence.

One of the practices I incorporate in my daily meditations to help me remember the illusory quality of life is **The Four Thoughts That Turn One's Mind to the Dharma.** They are:

- **Precious human existence.** This precious human birth, which is favorable for practicing the Dharma, is hard to obtain and easily lost, so I must make it meaningful.

- **Death, mortality, and impermanence.** The world and all its inhabitants are impermanent. The life of each being is like a water bubble. It is uncertain when I will die, and only Dharma can help me live and die more peacefully, so I must practice now with diligence.

- **The Law of Karma.** Because I create my own karma, I should abandon all unwholesome action. Keeping this in mind, I must observe my mind each day.

- **The problems of our normal conditioned existence.** Like a feast before the executioner leads me to my death, the homes, friends, pleasures, and possessions of this life cause me continual torment by means of the three sufferings (introduced before in the Basic Buddhist Teachings section). I must cut through all attachment and strive to attain right view and eventual enlightenment, or inner peace.

If we remind ourselves of these thoughts every day, we are less likely to attach ourselves to things we know are as impermanent and illusory as a bubble. What are these things? My meditation tells me it is everything we cling to as real: self, things, houses, jobs, health, relationships, systems of government and religion, absolute truths, and on and on.

The biggest of all these is the attachment to the illusion of self. We are attached to the self because it is the most real thing we know. It feels very much like something permanent and non-changing exists within us as our "self." But if we look closer, if we meditate on who this self is, we find it's not easy to clearly identify and point to the self that we identify with so strongly.

The Slippery Self

Sometimes we see our self as our body, sometimes as our mind, sometimes as our emotions. In Chapter 1, Verse 1 of *The Dhammapada* it says, "All that we are is the result of what we have thought: it is founded on our thoughts, it is made up of our thoughts."

We all know that our thoughts change constantly, so does our body, and so do our emotions. So, which of these is our self...and when? Right now? Today? Last week? Tomorrow? Only when I was an adult? Try to analyze this for yourself. Who is reading this right now, having this experience? Is it the same person who had a terrible day at work and felt trapped and depressed? Is the same person that went for a walk earlier in the day and felt free and happy? Which one is yourself?

Actually, it's not any one of these, but maybe all of them.

No-Self | Anatta

This introduces us to the concept of "no-self" or *anatta*. *Anatta* means that, rather than being a fixed, independent thing, we are much more like a process. And a relative process, at that. We all know that most of our concepts are relative, even if we cling to them as absolute. The concept of self is no different. Everything about your "self" is in a constant state of change and it is composed of many different changing things. It is essentially a system of relative processes.

According to this system, we are each comprised of five of these processes, or groupings referred to as aggregates or *skandhas*. The skandhas refer to the five aggregates of clinging or the five bodily and mental factors that contribute to our clinging and craving. They are form, feelings, perceptions, intentions, and consciousness. If you were to point to a self, the skandhas are as close as you can get. Just observe your thoughts and feelings for a few minutes and it will be quickly evident that you're on shaky ground when trying to claim anything like a concrete self.

Anatta is one of the "three marks of existence." The three marks are impermanence, unsatisfactoriness or suffering (dukkha), and No-Self or non-self (*anatta*). This is the conditioned existence I refer to. Our lives are made of certain conditions. We exist, of course, so that's the existence part, but the "conditions" part is that our life, our very existence has conditions on it. Just like a lease, rent, or purchase agreement. Everything's got conditions. Our lives do, too. You've been born into an existence that has the conditions of impermanence, some dissatisfaction, and a self that's elusive.

Yet anatta is not really no-self like there's nothing here. If I walk across this room and try to walk through the wall, that's not going to happen. I'm a self. I've got a body. I've got form. I have a self, but it's not the self I think it is. So, who are we? I did play with this a few paragraphs ago, but the concept is very slippery.

One thing I can guarantee in learning about Buddhism is that just when you think you've got a hold of one of these concepts, poof, it slips away like a greased pig. That slippery self, she ain't what you think she is!

Who Are You?

A quick exercise for you. Tell me who is your self? Okay. Do you have an answer?

Did you say your name? Did you say your occupation or your job title? Did you say your gender? Did you say your relationship status, as in mother, brother, father, or daughter? Did you say that you are human?

It's curious, isn't it? You really can't point to one single thing that is your core existence. The one single thing that would never change. All those other things: your gender, your job, and your relationship status will change. These are changing parts of you. It's kind of like pointing to the tires of a car, or the steering wheel, or the speedometer as the definition of a car. Or pointing to a Mazda and saying that is the definition of a car. But then what about a Ford?

I think most people, in answering that question, will start with, I'm an engineer or I'm a salesperson ... or they'll start by describing their relationships: I'm a father, I'm a sister, I'm a son. Or they might start describing their personality like I'm shy, or I'm an extrovert ... or their body type like I'm tall or thin or blonde with blue eyes.

But none of these things are who we are all the time, permanently. If that was so, then you as a child would not be you now, would she? Because if she was you as a child, then who are you now? That's the rub. There isn't one non-shifting thing about you. That is the concept of no-self.

In talking with people about Buddhism or in talking with coaching clients, one of the things that always stands out as a primary culprit in keeping people stuck or miserable is that they have a firm identification with some "me" or some self that they think they are. Over the course of my life—and by no means am I in the all-clear—I have "identified" as many people and each time I hung onto one of them as me, each time I clung to that self as me, I created my own little hells.

When I was a teen, I had a poetry "me," a righteous-indignation "me", and a reject-everything-and-anything "me".

As I got older, I stepped into an accomplishment-driven type persona that was me, but it was disguising the wounds of being gay in a world not ready to accept being gay openly, and the wounds of some bad relationships and resentments held from childhood.

And this led me to another me, a chronically ill me who fought the pervasive culture of wearing illness as another self with which to identify. Ultimately, this led me to plunge headfirst into the study of Buddhism, which was also led by the achievement-oriented or achievement-driven me that still hangs around me sometimes. The longer I studied and tried to achieve in Buddhism, the more confused I got. It was only when I stopped grabbing at it that it began to help. But that's a story for another book.

Which "You" Are You Clinging To?

So, let's talk about all these little mes. Dare I say Mini-mes? All the mes we cling to are just about as real as those little cartoon graphics. Like parts of my personal story, we probably all have wounded mes, wronged mes, sick mes, trapped mes, fired mes, and unemployed mes. So many mes; so much suffering.

Giving some person or characteristic a fixed name and identity is just a convention that humans came up with so we can talk about things with each other. The whole idea is a fiction. The problem is that as soon as we attach labels and concepts onto something, our egos kick in and start objectifying it, nailing it down, and spinning off stories to make something permanent out of it.

In a translation and commentary on the *Heart Sutra*, a smaller part of the *Prajnaparamita Sutra*, Rev. Gyomay Kubose (the father of my Sensei, Reverend Koyo Kubose of the Bright Dawn Center of

Oneness Buddhism) explains it as "we want to put a period on everything." In other words, we want to stop it. We want to fix it. "That's it. That's all."

And once fixed, we cling to our fixed concept as the truth, blinding us from any other truths presented to us even if they are also true. We want to put everything in neat little boxes so we can say, "Now I have it! Life is like this and I'm like this, and you're like that, and it will never change."

I do this too, of course, so I feel perfectly okay saying it's stupid, isn't it? No wonder we're so muddled.

As I mentioned before, that's what I see with coaching clients. When people start firmly identifying with some me or some self they think they are, then they have created their own prison. They may make some part of their life, one of their mes permanent, and guess what results from that? There's no way out!

If that me is miserable, formed by a story of who I should be ... or who I was before, but I'm not now ... or any other fantasy, then I have created my own suffering, my own hell because that is all I'll see. If someone plops a label on their shirt that says, "chronically ill," "victim," or "old and useless" then, of course, they respond accordingly, and it becomes a permanent condition.

But the good news is that there are no permanent conditions. You have a wonderful thing called a conditioned existence and one of those conditions is that nothing, in fact, is permanent, so rip that label off your shirt!

Quit repeating the same stories and see what's happening to you right now, at this very moment. Even chronic illness takes a day, hour, or a minute off, occasionally. But if we are busy listening to our thoughts telling us stories about how sick we will be tomorrow, that happy and feeling-good self will slip away.

In Gyomay Kubose Sensei's *Heart Sutra* commentary, he also added this: "So every day from morning to night, one thing after another." This seems simple, but it is the simplest things that can sometimes have the biggest impact. That line has had a huge impact on my life. I use that line as a mantra, "So every day from morning to night, one thing after another." It's to remind myself to wake up to what is happening right now and get out of the plans or endless, repeating stories that keep awareness kidnapped by my thoughts, stuck in my head.

This is the muddled, confused thinking that causes suffering or dissatisfaction to continue because we're not seeing what's happening at this very moment. We're not seeing clearly when we put on our victim, ill, older, or useless glasses. We've lost our ability to see clearly. We've lost our ability to see things as they are, from minute to minute. It is in the rare, clear-seeing minutes, the stories we tell ourselves will fade and things will naturally brighten, which explains why mindfulness or meditation is so important to our being happy or at least content.

This is not to imply that I am advocating magical thinking, a belief that if you don't refer to yourself as old, you won't be, or avoidance of the fact that you are getting older or that you have an illness. Not in the least. You may have a chronic illness. You may, in fact, be getting older. You may have been victimized, but what's going on right now? I'm also not telling you to adopt a passive, I-give-up attitude to life. What I'm suggesting is an opening up to what is happening at the moment, by not clinging to what you think it is or what you think they are, or what you think you are.

But you can't make yourself a clean, blank slate any more than you could make your mind a clean, blank slate when meditating. These are probably the two biggest misconceptions about Buddhism: that meditating is about stopping thoughts and

Buddhism is about stopping the self or not having a self. Instead, Buddhist practice is to make ourselves less obtrusive in everyday experience.

The practice is to not manipulate what's happening in each experience through reacting to what's happening, but, instead, just BE what's happening. It's not about what is happening to me, but what is happening. It's the activity of being. Being with no subject or object. Not I am angry, or I am hot, but I am. Instead of holding onto you and how you see what's not you, you just stand and be part of the experience. As paraphrased by Brad Warner, Dogen wrote "To study the self is to forget the self. To forget the self is to be experienced by the zillions of things. When experienced by the zillions of things, our own body and mind drop away."

Emptiness or Suchness | Sunyata

It's not just our sense of self that is like that, it's our sense of everything else, too. This is called sunyata, meaning emptiness or voidness, which is not to say everything is empty, in that it does not exist, it just doesn't exist the way you think it does. A loose quote from the *Lankavatara Sutra* is a favorite of mine: "Things are not as they seem, nor are they otherwise."

That's what *sunyata* is all about. It's all perception. It's all about "stars fading and vanishing at dawn, bubbles on a fast-moving stream, morning dewdrops evaporating in blades of grass, a candle flickering in a strong wind, echoes, mirages, and phantoms, hallucinations, and dreams."

It's all like a dream because it's all relative, dependent on other things and other people, and on its own causes—that is the meaning of interdependent. Nothing is real, as in concrete, fixed, unchanging, and permanent. Things are empty of those qualities because they are dependent on something else or are dependent on the way you view it, your perceptions.

So, despite the seeming emptiness of calling everything empty, it's exactly the opposite: it's full of possibility. It doesn't mean nothing exists; it means nothing exists as you thought it did, but it could equally exist as something else, far better. It all depends on your view and your intention, which is the second part of the "Awareness & Wisdom" chapter.

Right View Practice: No-Self & Emptiness

I will offer two small practices (actually, thoughts to play with) so that you can try to directly experience emptiness and emptiness of self. I say "try" because although Buddhas and many great Dzogchen or Mahamudra masters experience and continue to experience emptiness—have gone beyond and live in sunyata—I have only glimpsed it. Yet, in the trying, I get closer and closer to living in and from a place where concepts don't keep me anchored. And when not anchored to concepts, freedom emerges and offers the space of just living and experiencing, just being, and being aware of just being.

Nagarjuna, the Indian Mahayana philosopher said, "All is possible when emptiness is possible. Nothing is possible when emptiness is impossible." This is the "good news" of Buddhism.

Nagarjuna also posited the concepts of the Two Truths. I've written earlier about the problem with the word "truth" and the doctrine of Two Truths makes this even more apparent. The Two Truths are the ultimate truth and conventional truth. Ultimate truth is that everything is empty of being a discrete, permanent thing because everything is interdependent, everything is co-arising. This means that all things and all experiences arise dependently, not by their own power, but dependent on conditions that lead to their coming into existence.

Conventional truth is the truth of things in our everyday, walking-around existence. The truth of a table or a chair. We accept the table is there and it exists, but as we've discussed using the concept of emptiness, the table is a thing only because of its parts. It's empty of a "table essence." If you look for a table essence, or its inherent existence, you will find that it is dependent on the wood it is made of, the carpenter or factory worker who created it, the tree that the wood came from, and on and on.

The same is true of our self. We cannot point to one, discrete permanent self as our self. The body changes, the mind changes, our roles in interacting with others change. Which is the self? Conventional truth tries to define things as what they seem to be. But what is big? What is small? That depends on putting the big thing next to another thing and seeing if it is bigger. So, the big thing depends on something else for its "bigness". It is dependent.

And the other thought to play with, in your practice of emptiness, is to ask what makes one object what it is, as compared to another? What makes it what it is, as you label it? What is its essence?

Look around the room. Are the door and window the same? They both have a rectangular pane of glass. Are the grey squirrel and the chipmunk the same? They both have a bushy tail. What is the "doorness" of the door, the "windowness" of the window, the "squirrelness" of the squirrel, or the "chipmunkness" of the chipmunk?

Let your mind play with this concept. You may end up not being so sure of all the labels you put on everything.

Now, let's do the same thing with your concept of self. Try to find a picture of yourself when you were around two or three years old. Stare at the picture for a while. Do you feel as if you are looking at you? Do you feel yourself in that picture? Conventionally, you know that was you at that age. You remember how you looked from looking at pictures of yourself at that age.

Now, look at yourself in the mirror. Which one is you? The person in the photo or the person in the mirror? Are they both you? How can that be? You were the you in the picture at that time and you are the you in the mirror now. But both "yous" are dependent on something, right? Dependent on change. Dependent on time. When you were three you had blonde hair. Now you have grey hair. If your hair color is a concept you use to describe yourself and the color you use as a description of yourself is blonde, then you must not be you now, because you aren't blonde.

It's all very shaky, isn't it? The caution here is not to get stuck in thinking from the point of absolute truth or the point of conventional truth. These concepts are keys to seeing reality as it is. Thinking that things are permanent is incorrect but getting stuck in the concept of impermanence is not a good way to think either because it can foster a nihilistic view of life. This is what is meant by the middle way.

It is not that we don't have a self and things don't exist, but we don't exist, and things don't exist in the way we think they do. When you explore these concepts, you are entering into an expanded understanding of life as it is, which prevents you from clinging to seeing life as you would like it to be or that someone tells you it is. If you explore these thoughts deeply it is a form of meditation, analytical meditation, which can help lead you to longer and longer glimpses into *sunyata*.

The types of meditative practices I just illustrated can help loosen your mental grip on the rigid concepts of the way things are and, instead, allow you to freely experience things as they are, as experience arises and co-creates your reality with you.

Reflection on Right View

Essence of Light

Sun slips from behind ignorance
illuminating illusion,
but try to find it with your eyes
point even to its shadow,
with wisdom hidden
under your clothes,
inside your name.
But doing nothing,
being nothing,
a sage awakens darkness
penetrates the essence of light.

~ Wendy Shinyo Haylett

-2-

RIGHT INTENTION: REMEMBERING TO BE LESS OF A JERK

"May I think of every living being
As more precious than a wish-giving gem
For reaching the ultimate goal,
And so always hold them dear.

When I'm with another, wherever we are,
May I see myself as the lowest.
May I hold the other as highest,
From the bottom of my heart.

As I go through the day may I watch my mind,
To see if a negative thought has come;
If it does may I stop it right there, with force,
Since it hurts myself and others.

At times I will meet bad people,
Tormented by strong bad deeds and pain.
They are hard to find, like a mine of gold;
And so may I hold them dear.

Some jealous person might do me wrong,
Insult me, or something of the like;
May I learn to take the loss myself,
And offer them all the gain.

There may be times when I turn to someone
With every hope they'll help me,
And instead they do me great wrong;
May I see them as my holy guide.

In brief may I give all help and joy
To my mothers, directly or some other way;
May I take all the hurt and pain of my mothers
In secret upon myself.

May none of this ever be made impure
By the eight ideas of things;
May I see all things are illusion, and free
Myself from the chains of attachment."

— *"Eight Verses for Developing the Good Heart"*
by Kadampa Geshe, compiled by
Muchen Konchok Gyeltsen in the 14th century.

AS I MENTIONED EARLIER, I HAVE BEEN PREOCCUPIED WITH SELF-EXAMINATION AND INTROSPECTION SINCE I WAS VERY YOUNG. It was the drive for self-examination that hooked me on Buddhism. My first exposure to Buddhism came in the book *Studies in Zen* by D.T. Suzuki and the novel, *Siddhartha*, by Herman Hesse.

My intentions, at the beginning and during ongoing flirtations with the Dharma, were motivated by what I call "little" intention: A little intention is motivated primarily by selfish needs, wants, and/or immediate selfish gratification only. I came to the Dharma because I wanted my mind to be more peaceful. I wanted a way to minimize my worries and overcome a profound fear of death.

As I got older and more rooted in the culture and group-think within online and real-life Buddhist communities, I started to be a little more motivated by a desire to belong. A desire to be like everyone else who had a religion or the label of one.

Now, on the flip side of my confession, I can also share that my little intentions have, in part, changed to "big" intentions. My habitual selfish interests were slowly turned around, adjusted gradually—almost without my being aware of it. This process began with what I consider to be a profound blessing I received at my initial refuge ceremony on March 31, 2001.

On that day, at the end of the refuge ceremony, Lama Sonam Jorphel Rinpoche told me and my Dharma brothers and sisters, "Now your life has meaning." That simple phrase resonated in me like a temple gong. And it still rings to this day, whenever I get out of my "little self" long enough to hear it. It has ripened and changed me without me changing myself.

I think many people feel as though their lives can't be changed, or they have no power, or that their lives haven't really begun yet—like they are waiting for the right conditions—or that their lives are already over. So how do you feel about your life?

Is it motivated by a big story, something bigger than yourself and your own little ego-driven perceived wants and needs? Or is it motivated by renunciation (authentic becoming), loving-kindness, and correct view?

The Buddha offered his followers an opportunity to become part of a big story. It is a story of how afflictions are met with a noble response. Remember "noble" means a knowing or wise response. It is a story of how our own internal energies, which sometimes feel so destructive, can be transformed into a power that can create happiness and remove suffering in ourselves and other beings.

The correct view of self, or no-self to be exact, is critical to motivating right intent, or big intent. The big intent of Buddhism is ultimate compassion. His Holiness, The Dalai Lama, frequently says, "My religion is compassion." He also frequently quotes from Shantideva, "All happiness in this world arises from cherishing others; every suffering arises from self-cherishing." So, for me, this is the big intent, the thing that makes life meaningful and it requires that I maintain a focus on the right view of self.

However, as I emphasized earlier, just knowing what right view and right intention or big intention are, is different than acting on it. And the marvel—the preciousness of the Dharma—is that there are tried, tested methodologies given to us from many masters over more than 2,000 years that can help us practice. And if we do practice, the perfection of view, intention, and resulting actions are guaranteed!

One of my teachers illustrates the power and elusiveness of the good heart with a story from his life. He was on an airplane that appeared to be about to crash. He realized that everyone on the airplane was feeling the same terror: that they were all going to suffer and die in this horrible crash. If you're on a jet that's going to crash, any selfish interest seems like a waste of time and somehow you love all the people in the situation with you. But as soon as you get off the plane, of course, everyone starts rushing to be the first to get to the baggage claim. It's just like life. We're all in this life together and we're all hoping not to crash, not to suffer. And that, of course, is the situation we're all in, even if we're not on a crashing airplane because we are all suffering and dying.

The BIG Intention: The Good Heart

I talked about renunciation previously. Renunciation in Tibetan means "authentic becoming." It does not necessarily mean living in isolation from the world, but a renouncing of the delusions that keep one from becoming one's authentic self. And becoming one's authentic self means developing, or awakening, the Good Heart. And I don't mean excellent cardiovascular shape, although that is a good intention, too.

In Tibetan, compassion is translated as "nobility or greatness of heart" which implies wisdom, discernment, empathy, unselfishness, and abundant kindness. Remember that tender heart? We all had it as children, and I know some of you still have it: the unselfish urge to pick a daisy and hand it to a stranger; the drive to make sure everyone is happy. The perfect archetype of this great heart in the Buddhist tradition and Buddhist mythology is The Bodhisattva of Compassion or Chenrezig, (also known as *Avalokiteshvara* in Sanskrit, *Guanyin* or *Guan Yin* in Chinese, and *Kuan Yin* in Japanese). He/She is pictured in many forms with four or 1000 arms.

He is said to have made a vow to deliver all people from suffering and help them gain enlightenment and wished that if he ever hesitated to do that, he would split into a thousand pieces.

At one point he became discouraged by the great task and momentarily thought of giving up. At that instant, his head shattered into pieces. In his agony, he called out to Buddha Amitabha to help and Buddha Amitabha created a new body for him with 10 heads and 1000 arms, so that he could see and reach out to all beings and carry out his work more effectively.

It's a great story, but on a more profound level—where the everyday happens—it applies to this practice of right intention. We may have a noble intention but fulfilling it may prove too hard. However, if we keep the sincere motivation and continue, right intention allows a more powerful force to enter. If we can activate it in our consciousness and let it fight the function of the amygdala (the lizard-brain part of us that reacts in fear, anxiety, and aggression), it will slowly get stronger and start to guide our thoughts and actions.

That force is *Bodhicitta* or the wish for enlightenment for all beings. It is activated in our consciousness and begins to guide our thoughts and actions, reorganizing us. It transforms our view from a selfish view to the right view (essentially creating our 10 heads), which powers our activities and creates an endless capacity (1000 arms). So, in fact, *Chenrezig* is a symbol of our consciousness transformed and our ego shattered by *Bodhicitta*.

Intention is Remembering

The keywords in the subtitle of this chapter are "remembering", "less", and "jerk." The crucial part of having any intention—let alone a "right" one—is to remember that you have one! All too often, even if we do have an intention to do or to not do something, our habits or lizard brains kidnap us and we forget until the day is gone, or almost gone.

It's like resolutions. Speaking of remembering, do you remember the resolutions you made this year? And if you remember them, how have you done?

That's just it. Resolutions are thoughts only. Positive thoughts are great, but without action, the thought stays in your mind only briefly. The nature of thought is to arise and disappear. Thoughts aren't made of the stuff that keeps them around, inspiring action.

Resolutions typically don't work because they are only thoughts. They require another ingredient to work; they require mindfulness. It's like cleaning. There is rarely a cleaning product that works without some effort, some scrubbing on your part. Even products that claim to work like magic require a little effort, a little elbow grease.

This reminds me of a story from my childhood. I was probably around 10 or 12 years old. I was rinsing the supper dishes and putting them in the dishwasher, then I started to scrub the sink. There was a stain that I couldn't get out with the cleanser I was using. I yelled for my mom and asked her how to get the stain out.

She replied that I should use "elbow grease." I immediately opened cupboard after cupboard, looking for a jar ... a can ... a box

... **anything** that was labeled "elbow grease." Of course, I couldn't find it and, of course, it led to a few snickers among my parents and older siblings, but it's something I'll never forget.

So, elbow grease is a concept that pops into my head whenever I'm trying to do something and it's not working, I think, "elbow grease." It's a signal for me to put some focused effort and not go with my first whiny reaction that if it's not working, so it can't be done.

It's also a reminder that the solution starts and ends with me, despite the human intention to look everywhere out there for an answer or someone to blame. It doesn't always mean that I need to push harder physically or apply more force. Sometimes it does. But many times it's about focusing more intently on what's really happening. What's right in front of me and what needs to be done, then calmly considering what could work and how I might accomplish that. And, you know what? That takes a minute or two of being mindful and turning off the reactive brain that just wants to give up, be lazy, get mad, or blame it on someone or something else.

Let's go back to the stain in the sink. Sometimes, instead of picking up the sponge and applying a little elbow grease, I'm off on a mental conversation with myself that goes like this: "What the heck IS that stain? How did that get there? **Who** did that? And why didn't they notice it? Why didn't they clean it up? Now it's so much worse and so much harder to get out. If only they would ..." Maybe it's just me, but if you do that, too, remember the code words: Elbow Grease.

The trick to functioning more regularly from the Good Heart and letting *Bodhicitta* transform our actions is to remain aware of our big intention, our Good Heart, and have it guide us in the heat of any situation. Remembering our intentions can make us aware when these reactions are about to explode from us and provide a second to stop.

If you remember your intentions at the start of each day: whether to be more kind to a co-worker that annoys you or to speak more gently to your dog when she won't stop barking or poops in the house, then when a situation arises that triggers frustration or anger you will have a better chance of not unconsciously acting out of habit.

Equanimity is the ability to directly experience our emotions without totally giving in to and amplifying them, and without suppressing or denying them. Equanimity is a magic power that can reorganize you. The better you get at remembering and centering yourself in your intentions and, consequently, sidetracking habitual reactivity, calming fear, and quieting anger, the closer you get to developing equanimity.

It takes mindfulness and clarity to develop this magic power of equanimity. But it can transform our view from a selfish view to the right view, an unbiased view. It can, in fact, transform us into a being with 10 heads—not just a hair-trigger amygdala— that powers our activities and creates an endless capacity (our 1000 arms).

Taken from *The Thirty-Seven Practices of Bodhisattvas* is the all-important verse 36:

> *"In brief, whatever you are doing,*
> *Ask yourself, "What is the state of my mind?'*
> *Accomplish others' good—*
> *That is the practice of Bodhisattvas."*

Accomplishing your own and others' good is accomplished by getting to know what is going on in your mind. Give it a try and tell me what you think!

Intention is Remembering PLUS Action

I think if we honestly analyze our minds, most of us view intention as passive, as in the best intentions. As if it is accepted that our actions or activities won't be as we intended. "Oh well", we say, "she had the best intentions."

One of the key points to remember about Right Intention is that it implies action. It should not be a passive wish. The action can be motivated by a wish, but at the same time, you need to believe that the wish is a possibility and not some vague slogan.

You don't have to be perfect to be motivated by big intentions. You can fake it until you make it. You start by seeing yourself, your world, and all others as Buddha or Christ, which is what Vajrayana or Tantric practice is all about: Visualizing yourself as the person you wish to become. Any sports coach or music teacher will tell you the same thing. If you model yourself after your goal or your intended future state, then check to see if your thoughts and actions are consistent with that state, that model, and soon you will be shooting par or playing Bach Concertos.

But having a teacher does not guarantee you will be a professional golfer, pianist, or Buddha. You need to practice. You need to take the knowledge and the methodology your teacher gave you and make it your own. You need to act on the lessons.

You may hear this practice instruction from teachers of the Dharma: "Hear, think, and meditate." This is the action that is required to be a practitioner. I think most of us have a habit of hearing, then going to hear something else and something else again, creating a mental stew of good advice and precious teachings. Maybe with a little thinking thrown in. But what we tend not to do is to meditate on what we've heard and make it part of our lives, like practicing your golf swing every night in the backyard or playing scales on the piano every morning.

Plus, we need to see things as they really are—with Right View—to understand what our big intentions should be. Right View, as we discussed in the last chapter, is the first of the Eightfold Path and Right Intention is the second. But it is wisdom from Right view or right understanding that is the main support of the rest. Without wisdom, the structure crumbles.

This is how our mind works and the more we watch, the more likely we are to interrupt our thoughts *before* they kidnap us and make us do jerky things.

Right View Motivates Right Action

When coaching clients come to me complaining about their negative or unhelpful co-workers ... or complaining about being laid off 10 years and three jobs ago ... or complaining about recruiters, the job market ... whatever ... I put the focus back on them and have them see—clearly see—what they're thinking ... what they believe about what they're thinking ... then we go from there.

We are quick to blame everything "out there" for our problems. And, maybe, there is much out there (like the economy, the industry, the market, or your boss) that IS the cause of work and career problems. But maybe—just maybe—some of it is about you, too. Maybe there is fear, timidity, anger, or jealousy that robs you of the energy you need to reach your goals. Maybe it's procrastination, perfectionism, laziness, or boredom.

If you look, you will see. If you don't take a good look at yourself, you are only seeing half of the potential challenges to your goals and half of the potential strengths you can harness for success in reaching those goals.

Most of the time I think we all spend so much time "looking out there" for the elbow grease, that we don't even bother to think about how to scrub or even try to scrub the stain ourselves.

So, trying to be less of a jerk requires trying. Not just thinking but trying.

When we make a resolution (have the thought of doing something), our body (the action-making machine) tends to ignore it, because our body does what it is used to doing. In physics, we learn about inertia. The definition of inertia is: "A property of matter by which it continues in its existing state of rest or uniform motion in a straight line, unless that state is changed by an external force." Yep, it's a real thing demonstrated to us in our everyday behavior. That's why most resolutions aren't realized.

I was featured in an article by Eileen Hoenigman Meyer, "18 Career Resolutions to Make for 2018" in the career and company-review website, *Glassdoor*, where I said, "We typically have trouble self-correcting, because we do things habitually or from a reactionary pattern. We never actually see ourselves doing them until we complete the action. Being mindful is the process needed to accomplish change."

Gregg Krech, who wrote the book, *The Art of Taking Action: Lessons from Japanese Psychology*, says taking action is "doing what needs to be done when it needs to be done in response to the needs of the situation." Sounds simple, doesn't it? But most of the time we just react. We don't respond to the needs of the situation but instead, we respond to how we feel about the situation.

When we feel strong emotions or have an emotional response to a situation, it can prevent, kidnap, or distort our actions. Our emotions are wired in the limbic system of the brain. This is the flight-or-fight thing, our protective or survival mechanism. But the truth of most of our lives is that we really don't need that response most of the time. This flight-or-fight reaction performed by the amygdala activates and distorts or kidnaps our intentions. It happens fast and, before you know it, we're acting like a jerk.

"We didn't **mean** to," we say. We didn't **intend** to. Of course, we didn't but because we weren't watching our emotions—weren't aware—our amygdala fired and we acted like a jerk.

You need to honestly believe, to know that you can be better—be less of a jerk. I hear coaching clients, friends, family, and myself say things like this, "But this is how I am. I can't help it. I can't help being sarcastic; my whole family is sarcastic." Or "I can't help it that I just say things without thinking about them, that's who I am. I'm out there. I'm real."

When I hear those things ... When I hear myself say things like that, like my personal favorite, "I can't help that I'm judgmental ... or I can't help being a bit in-your-face." I try to stop and say, "Oh, YES YOU CAN!" You just don't want to apply any effort. You don't want to look at how that's really working for you. You don't want to apply any elbow grease!

The correct view of self, or no-self to be exact, is critical in the motivation of right intent or big intent. The big intent of Buddhism is ultimate compassion. This is the thing that makes life meaningful and it requires that we maintain a focus on the right view of self. But, as I emphasized earlier, just knowing what right view is, what right intention or big intention is, is different than acting on it.

The Buddha taught that there are **three kinds of Right Intention**, which counter three kinds of wrong intention:

- The intention of **renunciation** counters the intention of desire.

- The intention of **goodwill** counters the intention of ill will.

- The intention of **harmlessness** counters the intention of harmfulness.

Practicing the Good Heart: Mind Protection

There are many ways to practice activating big intention and ultimately, *Bodhicitta*. One is through chanting the mantra of Chenrezig, *Om Mani Padme Hum*, which you may be familiar with since it is in the popular consciousness and media. The symbol and sound Om (*Aum*), in Hindu philosophy, is said to reflect the primordial sound of the universe. It is used in Buddhist chant practices as the beginning and/or end sound of a chant.

Mani symbolizes the precious jewel or the precious jewel of wisdom and compassion. The "ma" syllable in *mani* is associated with dissolving attachment to fleeting pleasures. The "ni" syllable is believed to dissolve our attachments to desire and passion while cultivating our ability to be patient with ourselves and others. The entire word, *mani*, means jewel.

Padme symbolizes the lotus flower, which is the beautiful flower that blooms from the mud. The mud is our normal-walking-around little selves and little lives. Putting it together it means that the jewels of wisdom and compassion can blossom from us, but they **need** this mud of our little existence to blossom. "Pad" is the syllable that dissolves our attachments to our many prejudices and judgmental notions.

The "me" syllable helps dissolve our attachments to being possessive while also cultivating our powers of concentration. Together, *padme* means "lotus" and represents wisdom.

Hum is the invocation sound, which invokes the mind of Chenrezig. With the syllable, *hum*, we work to dissolve our attachments to aggression and hatred. We instead cultivate our own innate wisdom.

This mantra has a lot of meaning behind it. The one phrase that represents the mantra is: "The jewel is in the lotus," or "Praise to the jewel in the lotus." This is to say that within all of us is the lotus flower, it's just covered up by a lot of mud and icky stuff in our minds and in our life. Reciting this mantra with the right intention is believed to get rid of the mud and muck until we are as pure, compassionate, and wise as the lotus flower itself.

Mantra is literally a mind protector. So, if you are turned off by what seems to be so much "mumbo-jumbo" or magical thinking in this discussion on mantras, it really is a down-to-earth practice aligned with remembering right intention, the theme of this chapter.

Think of it as how to ingrain the thought of big intention and right view, instead of self-view and little intention. It is certainly a better substitute for most of the little thoughts that run through our minds constantly. And, if you want to add some visualization or feeling to the mantra practice, you can feel or imagine that you are calling on the blessings of *Chenrezig* and being infused with *Chenrezig*'s ultimate compassion.

His Holiness The Dalai Lama said that by chanting the *Chenrezig* mantra regularly you can transform your impure body, speech, and mind into the pure body, speech, and mind of a Buddha.

Right Intention Practice: Intention + Action

Three key concepts emerged in this chapter on right intention: a big story, meaning, or purpose; the intention to do something or try to do something aligned with the big story or purpose; and completing the intention through action. Intention in Buddhism is all of those things. Action without intention can easily be misguided, habitual, or worse. Intention without action is wishful thinking.

In Buddhism, to create the force of karma we need intent combined with deeds or action. Good intent plus good deeds contribute to good karma. Bad intent and bad deeds contribute to bad karma. Our legal system uses similar criteria. It is not enough to have committed an illegal act, but the intent to commit the act must also be proved to establish guilt and determine the type of sentencing.

Don't freak out about my mention of karma. You do not have to subscribe to a belief in rebirth to understand and accept the workings of karma. Karma is, essentially, the consequences of actions and intentions.

But which is more important? Actions or intentions? Without thinking too deeply, I believe most of you would answer actions. And many times in this book I stress the importance of acting on our intentions, since intention alone is only a wish. Yet, without the proper or right intention, action is reaction. A practice of purposeful intention can condition us to carry out actions that we wish to carry out. No empty wishes unfulfilled and no regrets over reactions not intended.

We can take vows that keep our hearts and heads aligned with how we would like to act or the type of person we would like to become or something less formal like establishing a daily practice that aligns our thinking with our true intentions. So, rather than rushing out the door to work with the news blaring or responding to a Facebook post with coffee in hand, maybe there is more we can do?

What are some of the ways you can think of to reinforce your good intentions? What practices or habits could help you spread good intentions through the world?

My suggestion for a right intention practice is to adopt and build a habit of "Everyday Gassho", a practice created by Rev. Koyo Kubose, my Sensei with the Bright Dawn Center of Oneness Buddhism. I began this practice in 2012 as part of a commitment to completing the 21-Day Daily Dharma Program. When a Bright Dawn lay minster colleague and friend suggested I begin this practice to start incorporating more spiritual ritual in my life, I scoffed a bit at how simple it seemed. Yet, I began the Everyday Gassho practice, completed the 21 days, and I am still doing it today. I discovered it was anything but simple in building a habit and establishing a practice that joined a big intention with a small, daily action.

This simple practice became a powerful part of my life. I attribute that power to the combination of a purpose or intention bigger than myself with the fulfilling of it in a planned or habitual action, even a seemingly small action. Will my two daily gasshos lead to world peace or saving the planet? Probably not directly, but they will keep me aligned with my own good intentions and bigger purpose, which should help make me a better person every day. I believe it can do the same for you.

The Everyday Gassho practice and an article on "Why Gassho", written by Rev. Koyo Kubose, is included below:

Everyday Gassho Introduction

The act of Gassho is done by putting the palms of your hands together in front of your heart and bowing your head. Gassho may be done sitting or standing, with eyes closed or open, and with or without meditation beads. As part of the 21-Day Program, a Harmony Gassho and Gratitude Gassho are done daily in front of your home altar or Special Place of Tranquility, also known as SPOT.

Harmony Gassho

The Harmony Gassho is done in the morning and sets your motivation for the day. Choose a time when it will best fit into the flow of your usual morning routine. If helpful, post a "Gassho" reminder sign in a visible place. One suggestion is to do your morning Harmony Gassho just before breakfast. As an aid to making Gassho a habit, you can mentally make eating breakfast contingent upon first doing Gassho. No Gassho, no meal. Keep a planner, calendar, or app to record the completion of your morning Harmony Gassho.

The verbal recitation accompanying your morning Gassho can be the word "harmony." In lieu of any other strong considerations, it is suggested you use the recitation "harmony" during your initial 21-Day Program. Other recitations can be introduced later. Your recitation can be spoken with any degree of loudness or simply be said to yourself. The depth or power of the recitation is facilitated through your breath. After a moderately deep (but not overly long) inhalation through your nose, make your recitation as you exhale through your mouth. The sound of the last syllable should be extended until the end of the exhalation. As an approximate guideline, your inhalation can be about 3-5 seconds long, whereas your exhalation should be about

9-15 seconds long. Keep your body and head erect as you inhale. As the last syllable of the recitation is finished, slowly bow your head, keeping your hands and body still. At the end of the recitation, most people like to stay in the finishing position for a while (perhaps for 1-3 normal breaths) so that you don't get the feeling of rushing off immediately after the recitation.

The preceding is a description of a standard or basic procedure; other variations can be developed later after the initial 21-day period. Other than doing the one recitation, there isn't a recommended number of additional recitations you should do. More is not necessarily better but if desired, you can do more than one (although it probably is not a good idea to do more than three at a given time).

The underlying sentiment of the Harmony Gassho is that you will try your best to have a spirit of cooperation with others, and always be as calm and patient as possible. The seed of this sentiment will gradually blossom into an understanding that can be called wisdom.

Gratitude Gassho

The Gratitude Gassho is done in the evening and recaps your day. It is suggested that you do it just before eating dinner, again mentally making eating contingent upon first doing Gassho. On days you eat out, you can do your Gratitude Gassho just before going to bed. Perhaps a "Gassho" reminder note near your bed would be helpful. Immediately after doing your Gratitude Gassho, note it in your calendar or planner.

Use the same procedure as described for the Harmony Gassho except that your recitation is the word "gratitude." The underlying sentiment accompanying the Gratitude Gassho is an awareness of interdependency—that you are supported by nature, by other people, by everything. There is a feeling of "counting your blessings," of "grace," or "how grateful I am." The seed of this sentiment will naturally blossom and be expressed in compassionate ways.

Everyday Gassho

Putting your hands together in Gassho can be broadened to include different creative hand gestures that can be related to a variety of themes or everyday activities. You are encouraged to discover or create your own Gasshos.

The Bright Dawn Center of Oneness Buddhism publishes a quarterly newsletter, *Oneness*, and in each publication, there is a column called "YES: Your Everyday Spirituality." The column is formatted for the three months of the current season, describing a creative Gassho to use as practice for each month.

In the current issue the Gassho for October is "Falling Leaf Gassho" and the theme is "Autumn Maple Leaf." The purpose is "Living a Natural Life" and the method is: "Start with a one-handed Gassho, then slowly twist your wrist back and forth as you lower your hand to waist level. Liken this movement to how an Autumn maple leaf falls, showing front, showing back. Try to live such a natural life, without artificiality or pretensions!"

Important Considerations

You may already be familiar with Gassho and perhaps you're wondering why it is such a big deal. You may even think that Gassho is something simplistic and perhaps narrow in scope and effect. However, the Harmony and Gratitude Gassho as previously described are only a beginning. They are two handy tools for your spiritual tool bag. There are many more tools or different kinds of Gassho that can be added to your spiritual tool bag.

As you add tools such as Gassho, your spiritual path will become deeper and richer as your awareness of the many ways we act without thinking—without intention—intensify. Adding intention to even simple everyday practices like Gassho can make it a profound spiritual practice that deepens your understanding of Buddhist teachings and heightens your appreciation and awareness of life and the people around you.

Many people need to be liberated from the idea of spiritual practice as only being practices authorized and approved by some authority. There is definitely a place for the time-tested traditional rituals handed down through a particular lineage. These rituals need not be rejected. It is not a matter of advocating that something is taken away but rather of adding something.

Modern spirituality requires flexibility of attitude in order to internalize and make the ancient truths relevant to each of us. Spirituality is individual and personal. Individual creativity in spiritual practice does not have to be viewed as an egotistic act that threatens established ways of doing things. You can give yourself permission to express yourself and be creative in the application of traditional or established practices. Growth means being open to change, both for individuals and institutions. If a particular traditional way works for someone and nothing else is desired, this is fine too. It is not necessarily an either/or situation when it comes to your personal spiritual path. Do what works for you and don't judge others who are doing things in other ways.

Being non-judgmental is of great value in living life with inner peace and in harmony with others. Diversity in spiritual paths is okay. You may start out in a narrow, sectarian tradition and by following this path in-depth, your spirituality may mature and come to be expressed in very open, liberal ways. Conversely, you may start out exploring many different individualized spiritual paths and, as a result, come to settle on one particular way as the best for you.

All paths have value because what is of value depends on time, place, and person. The word value is being used here not with regard to religious truth or teachings themselves but rather how you access, apply, or express such truth or teachings. It is important to examine the assumptions you might have about the nature of spirituality and spiritual practice. Such examination is especially helpful when you feel you aren't making progress spiritually. When spiritual growth does take place, your assumptions about the whole process often undergoes change too.

Whatever spiritual path you are on, keep a "beginner's mind." Don't get overly attached to your answers and conclusions. At the same time, remember that no matter what happens, nothing is wasted. All your experiences have their place in your spiritual journey. Enjoy the journey itself; the journey is not just a means to get to a destination. Don't ever think you have arrived. Keep going, keep going. Just be sincere, and don't forget to laugh.

Reflection on Right Intention

Full Bloom – Lilac

Each year you create yourself
out of gnarled gray wood—
flashes of purple on first green—
your sweet essence rises
after the dew and barely lingers
until evening breezes incite
my awareness of you.

Some years I barely notice
the sensation you are—
trapped inside my gray brain—
nurturing the black and white
of each scentless thought
in some misguided belief
that I am the miracle.

~ Wendy Shinyo Haylett

PART TWO:
ACCEPTANCE · ETHICS

–3–

RIGHT SPEECH: ZIP IT!

"The purpose of a fish trap
is to catch fish,
and when the fish are caught
the trap is forgotten.

The purpose of a rabbit snare
is to catch rabbits.
When the rabbits are caught,
the snare is forgotten.

The purpose of the word
is to convey ideas.
When the ideas are grasped,
the words are forgotten.

Where can I find a man who has forgotten words?
He is the one I would like to talk to."

— Chuang Tzu

IF YOU THOUGHT RIGHT VIEW AND RIGHT INTENTION WERE A CHALLENGE, RIGHT SPEECH IS THE MOST DIFFICULT OF ALL—not difficult to understand, but difficult to accomplish.

Because it is the most difficult to accomplish, I think it is our most important daily practice. Especially in this age of speech at the speed and interconnectivity of the Internet, where words are thrown around like the empty promises of a politician in an election year. Although it's worse than that. They're thrown around without a second thought about who could be affected; who could be hurt. It's the lizard brain of the amygdala in action again.

Reflect for a minute: Other than thinking, what do you spend most of your time doing, in your active waking hours? Talking. We're always talking. Even when we're listening, we're talking—mentally creating our responses. Our thoughts can be considered speech, as well. We tell ourselves stories about ourselves and others all the time. We have a constant running narrative in the head.

Back before the Internet, a time that some of you may not even remember, we still talked all the time. Gossiping with our co-workers and neighbors. But now with texting and the endless social media forums, it's a constant stream of yap, yap, yap. Sharing our opinion of everything with everyone.

The constant social media opinionating reminds me of something Andy Warhol said in 1968: "In the future, everyone will be world-famous for 15 minutes." It's like we really think everyone is waiting for—or needs to hear—our opinion on whatever: the weather; Presidential scandals and international conspiracies; the GOP; the Democrats; the economy and tariffs; gun violence; the latest stupid stunt some movie, TV, or music star committed ... and on and on.

Since when are we meteorologists, political analysts, sociologists, psychologists? Yet we seem to think we have an informed opinion on everything! Whenever I'm tempted to spout off on something like that, I stop and say, "*Really???* Who cares what YOU think??" My stop mantra is a combination of what I just said: "Who cares what you think?" And "What do you really know about this subject (whatever it is ... fill in the blank) anyway?"

Admittedly, these stop-before-you-spout mantras don't always work for me. Sometimes I still spout. And I must admit that I feel a little uncomfortable exposing my hypocrisy. But that's what this book is all about: Sharing the struggle, connecting with you at the level of the struggle, and giving you some tips and tricks that I've used to make my life a little easier, a little happier—hopefully, so you can be a little happier, too.

In 2017, I took a personal vow to not share my opinion about anything on the Internet, unless it was a positive, inspiring message. I took the same vow a few years earlier, also during a time of hot political debate. The first time I made the vow, I didn't do so good. The second time, I did much better and I've stuck to keeping it zipped (most of the time anyway!). And when I screw up, I feel an aversion to my own wrong speech. That's the best deterrent there is.

The good thing is that I'm quick to notice and self-correct now. It's like one of my teachers always said: You can check to see if your practice is working by seeing if the length of time between having a thought and acting on it gets shorter. When you first start practicing, the time span might be a day or so before you feel regret for wrong speech. But the length of time gets shorter and shorter if you stick to it.

Language is a conceptualization, and by its nature, it discriminates, separates, labels, and judges. Speech conceptualizes external things. It cements or reifies internal thoughts, feelings, and events into self-existent external things. Those thoughts and feelings become a discrete "type" rather than a mere moment where senses or circumstances coincide to produce a thought, feeling, or event.

My spouse says this: "anything after the words 'I am' is a lie." That is true. And, if practiced, is the most direct practice of the combination of right view **and** right speech possible. Because you are entirely empty of anything after "I am."

Speech, as we use it, is primarily an offensive weapon of the ego or its defensive armor. Speech is a direct expression of grasping to a sense of self, to a discrete identity. We promote this "me-ness" with our words and further reinforce our own view of separateness and disconnection from the happiness and suffering of others.

Every time we hear ourselves talk about what is happening to us we shore up that false division. Sometimes it seems that when we are driven to speak, the impulse that drives the speech is a state of mind that is not positive and does not hold right intention or right view.

We all have had the experience of feeling hurt by something someone did or said to us, followed by a compulsion, a burning need, to tell someone about it immediately. Which, of course, focuses the mind of the speaker and the listener on the concept of the other person as bad. And that builds the concept of you as a good person, who was wronged, and now is justified in your use of wrong speech.

Many Dharma teachers instruct their students in the application of right speech by encouraging them to never talk about anyone—whether good or bad—if that person is not there to hear. If you try to do that as a practice, you will quickly observe that we spend far too much time talking about other people. Every time we do, we are alienating ourselves from the present. If the person is not there, then we must be talking about something in the past, right?

And, taking it even further, this habit of talking about others alienates us from right intention, because we are conceptualizing the person, painting a picture with words—based on our thoughts—rather than actual causal experience.

The concept of right speech is not only Buddhist advice. It is found in all great teachings. Jesus said that it isn't what goes into your mouth that defiles you, but what comes out of your mouth that defiles you.

Don Miguel Ruiz, who wrote of ancient Toltec wisdom in his book, *The Four Agreements*, said: "If we can see it is our agreements which rule our life, and we don't like the dream of our life, we need to change the agreements." His primary agreement is to "be impeccable with your word." Ruiz calls it the most important and the most difficult to honor. He says your word is your creative power, a force that creates the events in your life. He says we "cast spells" on ourselves, and each other, with our word.

I love the concept of the value of listening being higher than the value of speech, as indicated by the fact that we have two ears and only one mouth. I think about that a lot.

When I first started practicing in the Tibetan tradition, it was pointed out to me how the representations of Buddhas and bodhisattvas in art have very large ears and much smaller mouths. Check it out sometime. Get on Google and do a search for Buddha and Bodhisattva images and look at those ears! In Western culture, small ears close to the head are thought to be the most beautiful, but in the Orient, large ears are looked upon as auspicious because they indicate wisdom and compassion.

Interesting, huh? If our current culture was represented by what we do and what we value, we would look like emoticons: all mouth and no ears. Emojis don't have ears! This is a great contrast of images to keep as a motivator. Do you want to be more like an emoji or a bodhisattva?

Now that I've got your attention about how important this third path is, it's time for me to come clean.

The Four Restraints

When I was in third grade, I won the "Chatty Cathy" Award. And unless you're my age, you probably don't get the reference to Chatty Cathy. Chatty Cathy was a doll made by Mattel in the 1960s. It used the cutting-edge technology of the time: a phonographic record inside the doll. If you pulled the string on her back, she talked, despite her lips not moving. She said things like "I love you" or "I hurt myself!" or "Please take me with you" or "Let's play school" or "May I have a cookie?"

About my award. It wasn't a good thing. I was talking in class and the teacher made me wear a sign all day (and all the way home) that said, "Chatty Cathy." Looking back, I think the teacher wasn't exhibiting skillful means in ostracizing me by making me wear a sign all the way home. It had an effect on me. It probably stopped me from talking in class for a period of time, but it didn't do much to alter my life-long love of talking.

I was using wrong speech as a third-grader—too much speech—or idle speech. And I continue to use wrong speech every day and, probably, many times a day. Before you think that I lie or swear constantly, I will point out that it is subtler than that. And once I completely come clean you might see how much you might confess to yourself.

My first confession is that I'm a talker. I love to talk, and it comes quite naturally in all situations, with all people. That can be a good thing: I can make pleasant conversation with almost anyone. But sometimes I should shut up. My mother told me when I was young that I inherited her gift of gab. My father used to comment, "You sure can talk." As you can see, to some it is a gift, to others, a questionable trait.

There is a set of ten vows in Buddhism, referred to as the Ten Non-Virtues or The Freedom Vows. They are grouped by the three gateways (body, speech, and mind). Of the ten, three are related to the body, three are related to the mind, and four are related to speech.

The four things that you should watch for are these restraints and their antidotes for practicing right speech:

- Refrain from lying; practice **truthful** speech;

- Refrain from divisive talk; practice **peaceful** speech;

- Refrain from harsh words; practice **gentle** speech;

- Refrain from idle talk; practice **meaningful** speech.

Truthful Speech

Being truthful, in an impeccable way, is a lot more difficult than not telling a lie. Truthful speech means just not lying, but not giving someone—or ourselves—the wrong impression. We do that all the time don't we? We purposely give people impressions that we're more in control, less fearful, more positive, happier, healthier—whatever.

And how do we do that? With our words. We carefully leave words out or choose particular words to have a certain effect. We don't even think about it; it's natural—almost an instinct.

We also talk untruths by posting on Facebook and other social media platforms. We see it all the time. So much so, we hardly even notice anymore. Images of the beautiful dinner someone just made or their Fitbit 40,000-step status. Posts commenting on our accomplishments.

Is it lying? Not really. Is it truthful? Also, not really. The stories we tell with our spoken words or with our social media image uploads or posts are based on grasping to outcomes we want or want others to think we have actually accomplished. There is nothing wrong with having goals or intentions. But if we share these things with everyone, what are we doing? (Let's face it, are all your Facebook friends really your friends?) It's giving the impression—whether consciously intended or not—that this is who we are and what we do all the time. That beautiful vegan meal photo you posted is one meal. Did you post a pic of the meal you quickly grabbed on the way between work and a meeting the day before? You know. That one.

I know I have manipulated impressions. I've implied I understood something someone was saying even though I was hopelessly confused, just to get out of the conversation. I have posted photos of my beautiful and neat vegetable garden at the beginning of the season and not posted the tangled web of cucumber vines choking out tomato plants in August—a testament to an inadequately planned garden space instead of the "master gardener" photo from early summer.

It's not even completely conscious. I have had to make a concerted effort to be conscious of what I'm about to say or about to post on social media. So, what's the harm in it, right? My intention is not really to deceive, right?

The harm is that it's based on wrong view and wrong intention. Every time we purposely leave a false or inflated impression, or utter a word that is not totally—impeccably—true, we are trying to fool others and trying to fool ourselves as well. But it doesn't really fool ourselves and it's wrong view. It demonstrates a belief in dual concepts as truth. And it's clearly wrong intention when we are posing or leaving a more positive impression on others than we know to be true.

Pretending to behave in ways we don't really behave is a lie we tell ourselves, yet we don't believe it. We know it's not true, so it compromises our peace of mind while creating a false image for others. Like a boomerang, this lie—even if it's not done purposely—comes back at us, disturbing our peace. And, if others really believe our false images, then we have also potentially caused another to suffer.

It sounds complicated, but the simplest explanation is this: if we speak something not aligned with right view, not aligned with things as they really are, then we keep fooling ourselves about how things really are. We are hiding from, or escaping from reality, which only fools ourselves. And it is obviously wrong intention, because every time you allow someone to have the wrong impression about you, your intention was what? To confuse? To lie?

This reminds me of the this poem by Ryokan, a Zen monk and poet:

> *Maple leaf*
> *Showing front*
> *Showing back*
> *Falling down*

That's what we do when we give the wrong impression; when we don't speak all the truth about ourselves; when we don't share the truth of who we are—our naturalness—we are showing only front.

Being attached to words—yours or others—can prevent right seeing, right view. Words can point. They can point the wrong way or the right way. Either way, you are the one that must find the way. Deliberately pointing the wrong way is only going to keep you hopelessly lost.

This may not seem like a big deal. After all, everyone does this all the time. Yep, that's true. But every time you do this, you begin to devalue the truth of who you are, who others are, and the truth of things as they are.

Sure, you can fool people. They won't know the difference, but, as one of my teachers said, "if you're going to do something you know is wrong, you might as well do it with the door open" because you are the one creating your own karma; it's not about being caught by some external judge.

Peaceful & Gentle Speech

The next practice is to refrain from divisive talk and harsh words, which means to use peaceful speech. What is peaceful speech? Refraining from harsh, critical, judgmental, impatient, and annoying speech.

Like my social media vow. In making slips, I noticed that it wasn't that I posted blatantly hateful comments or aggressive, in-your-face quote-sharing, but the subtle ones that proudly declare me as something or wave my allegiance/belief in something, or sarcastically poke fun at "the other side."

Yet, I think those are even worse. They masquerade as harmless support for a cause (and, consequently, a stand against one) and can seduce you into thinking what you're doing is not divisive, but informative. But, then there's that tiny tinge of smug self-righteousness you feel when you post it.

What is that?

It is rejoicing in your "otherness." We make "others" out of people who don't think like us, don't believe like us, don't live like us, and don't love like us. Yet, I am someone else's "other." It is a self-perpetuating misadventure that divides acquaintances, friends, family members, churches, states, countries, and the world. And, as much as I love the Internet, Facebook, and social media in general, they can be particularly conducive to participating in acts of mindless divisiveness.

Every time we share a strongly one-sided political or religious link to a news article, editorial, or blog we are declaring we "are" something or stand for something and, therefore, we create a potential border or separation between us and others.

Granted, sometimes you just have to share some positive bit of news that you are happy about or something that is truly informative. I think that is great and one of the joys of Facebook: being able to rejoice in others' happiness, if it's not information you are sharing to change minds to your side.

Do we have to keep waving our flags of belonging over and over again? I am guilty of this and it is nothing other than tribal behavior, which by its nature, is dualistic and divisive. Let's face it, after one or two of these postings, most of our Facebook friends already know how we feel about things and "what side we're on." After that, isn't our motivation trying to get those who don't share our beliefs to finally see the light and come over to our side?

I am particularly offended by the divisive nature of those poke-fun-at postings I see routinely on Facebook. These are the ones sharing the latest political or religious bashing jokes, satires, cartoons, and videos from Late Night talk/comedy. I may even find them funny if I am on the right side, but, if not, it feels downright mean-spirited.

Facebook, Internet chat groups, and social media make it very easy to be snarky—or even downright abusive—in ways we wouldn't dream of doing face-to-face or on the phone. I think we would agree that we would never tell a born-again joke at a dinner party or business meeting, in the presence of someone we know to be an evangelical Christian. Yet, do we even stop to think that that's what we're doing with some of the things we post on Facebook?

John Suller, a psychology professor at Rider University, says that Internet users readily fall prey to what Suller calls the "online disinhibition effect." Suller says the medium itself drives us to act out in ways we normally wouldn't because "people experience their computers and online environments as an

97

extension of their selves...an extension of their minds...and therefore feel free to project their inner dialogues...into exchanges with others."

I have witnessed this myself: during election cycles, debates over Supreme Court rulings, and dialogue or argument about potential legislation. I have been shocked by unexpected angry and vocal reactions from people I thought I knew who posted angry links or gave "likes" to aggressive, sarcastic, and angry thoughts on both sides of an issue.

It made me question my own posting behavior and encouraged me to renew my vow to question each thing I am tempted to post or like, before I do so, as a test to see if it is something I would say directly to anyone I've allowed to view my posts. Since I renewed that vow, I have stopped myself many times.

Think about it. Think about what you are about to post, like, or dislike on social media before you do so. Take a minute. Take a breath. Better yet, sleep on it.

Most importantly, reflect on the words you use that could offend or make others feel uncomfortable. If you feel this doesn't apply to you, which I might do if I were reading this, stay with me here as I make another confession about not using gentle speech, which I tend to do quite regularly.

I've struggled with not using gentle speech. The third of the Four Restraints are actually about refraining from using harsh words. Yet, what seems harsh to me may not seem harsh to you and what seems harsh to you may not seem so to me. Our lives condition us in certain ways. The way we were brought up, the people we work with, the movies or TV we watch, the music we listen to. All these things can condition us to be numb to or ignore certain words or tones of voice. If we're used to using a certain bad word or used to loud talking, it seems normal to us and not the least offensive. To someone else not used to it, it can seem harsh.

Using a "bad" word and talking loudly are both things I've done and tried to stop doing. One of my Buddhist teachers, one of my Unitarian minister friends, and many of my Buddhist friends admit to the problem, too. It's difficult to find anyone that doesn't occasionally utter a bad word. There are lots of them ... and it is culturally accepted to use them. And if you work in a normal Western work environment, watch current TV shows and movies, and listen to current popular music, it is even more likely one of these has found its way into your regular vocabulary.

For many years, I worked in broadcast television as an engineer. I was one of the first women engineers and I found myself, at 19, working among men. I grew up in a family of three brothers where talking loudly, verbal sparring, and arguing was part of daily life. My vocabulary was colorful, my tone of voice was quick to be loud, sharp, and direct if needed. Gentility was something I witnessed in other families and life situations, but it was not something I culturally appropriated.

It has taken many years to see these things about my speech and many more to try to restrain from harshness. The good news is I am getting better at breaking the habit. I'm not perfect, but practice does help.

One of my teachers admitted to using questionable speech as a part of his teaching style. And, I, too, admit that those words fly out of my mouth when I'm going for effect. But why? What is the effect we're seeking? This is how I've tried to train myself. What is it I want to express? What feeling do I want to share? Who is hearing me? Would another approach be better? Admittedly, this is a lot to ask yourself in that second before something comes rushing from your mouth. But if you even try to ask one of those questions, it might reorient you to your listener and their expectations or sensibilities.

My mother, who died 22 years ago, had a wonderful, open humanness that was her very essence. She used to jokingly say her favorite word was "shit." People laughed, and my mother used it as her special explosive expletive—her special word of frustration—and guess what? Now, of course, it comes flying out of my mouth every time I stub my toe, drop something, or make a mistake on a work project. But couldn't it as easily be "rats" or "sheeesh?" My father-in-law used to say "gads." Even when he was golfing and he blew an easy putt, he would say "gads" in frustration. It might have been a loud gads, but it was still only gads. I like that.

Gentle speech is speech that brings people together rather than dividing them. It is helpful, compassionate, and considerate of people's feelings. Speaking in ways that bring people together is opposite to our normal human tendency. We tend to divide others, in order to bring people around to our side, attaching ourselves to expectations. We say, "did you hear what he said about you?" Or we ask if someone heard about a stupid thing some politician said when we know for a fact the person we are talking with voted for and supported him.

I am also guilty of divisive speech. Many years ago, I jumped on the bandwagon to gossip about a professional associate. I'm not sure why, maybe I wanted to reassure myself that I was right in feeling anger or frustration with this person, so the longer the group talked about her, the better I felt? I don't know. Maybe at some level, it was about wanting the group to like me more or to seem more a part of the team? Many times, I think we gossip to be liked. I honestly don't know why I do it, and I know it's wrong for me to do because it cannot help my situation, theirs, or the person being gossiped about.

The media that surrounds us is full of divisive speech. Social media, cable news, talk shows, reality TV, radio talk, whatever. It's all about exposing how bad, how wrong, how stupid, how illegal, how liberal, how conservative someone or some group is, in hopes of generating a response that's evoked from a coliseum-like mob mentality. "We gotta get 'em!"

It's news, it's not journalism, but it gets ratings. Absurd as it seems to most, it seeps into our consciousness like poison gas or a virus in an email attachment. We don't think we're affected until we feel ill or the computer won't boot up. Even if we don't watch or read the stuff, people around us are talking in the same divisive language. Just listen, get familiar with it, and ask yourself if you do it, too. You will be surprised how much divisiveness you don't even pay attention to anymore! It's in your mind, somewhere —and remember—your mind is what creates your world.

Meaningful Speech

The next practice is to speak meaningfully or refrain from idle talk. It's about making sure what you're saying has relevance to you or the person you're speaking to. That automatically disqualifies talk about celebrities, the problems of political figures, the private life of a sports star, how much weight a mutual friend gained ... and a whole lot of what we all talk about every day!

One of my teachers explained idle talk as "willingly and happily engaging in wasteful conversations about sex, crimes, war, and politics." That pretty much describes the kind of media chatter and conversation America wakes up to, goes to sleep to, eats lunch and dinner to, and works to every day.

Remember playing the telephone game when you were a child? One child whispers a sentence in the ear of another, and that child whispers to the next child, and on and on until the communication of the sentence goes around the circle of children and comes out on the other side, a completely changed message. That's what we do when we gossip or happily engage in idle chatter. I know I do it. I've jumped right into a conversation about a political situation or person—especially if I'm not that pleased about the situation or person—and exaggerate the negatives.

Getting in on that kind of talk triggers some sort of internal response. Some thrill. Sort of how anger is exhilarating and awful at the same time. That darn amygdala again. It's like we love to get ourselves and the people around us all worked up about whatever the subject is. I do it and I see that many of my friends and associates do the same thing. Why? How does that mess with our good intentions, our purpose?

Talking robs you of focus on your intention, your concentration, and your energy. Anyone who has had the experience of creating something understands this. In the planning stages of a creative work: a poem, painting, or even a new business idea, we instinctively protect that creative energy by not speaking of it until the plan or artwork becomes fully formed in our mind, because we know it will leak too much of the energy we need to make it happen.

The guideline we should follow should be to talk only from a sense of purpose, either a smaller purpose or a larger, more universal purpose. We should speak when there is a purpose for us to speak. If it can help someone, or they need to know, and it won't hurt them—that seems like a good guideline to follow.

The direct result from Right Speech is meaningful communication that is naturally friendly and amiable towards others. The Buddha said, "if one cannot say something useful, one should keep 'noble silence'." An example of noble silence is a story about a Roshi (Zen master) and his student enjoying a beautiful morning. The student says: "What a beautiful morning." The Roshi responds: "Yes, but what a pity to say so."

Right speech is really more about listening than speaking, but not the kind of listening that most of us do. You know that listening. Someone is telling a story or relaying some information and you are only partially listening, the rest of your mind is formulating a response, another story, a better fact, supporting evidence—whatever.

What does that say about your intention? When you're formulating your response, what is your intention? Is it to one-up, out-do, challenge? Unless it is pure support for them—as you would want to be supported—is a response even necessary?

Pay attention to how you listen when others are talking.

Both Native American and Zen teachings use the term "bear witness." Bearing witness is about experiencing life as it is. Not as you would like it to be, colored by your expectations—but as it is. Bearing witness to our lives in every second is a wonderful practice. Bearing witness is a subtle aspect of right speech. It is about accepting reality just as it is, with no need to add on with your own two cents or "buts". That reality or "suchness" just is.

In our current culture, speaking of things as if what is wished for is true—a sort of magical thinking that we can speak things into existence as a demonstration of positivity or an act of faith has become commonplace. It seems to have come out of a jumble of New Age and positive psychology thinking that, at first glance, seems harmless and possibly even helpful, but in the end, proclaiming that things are or will be other than they are is a lie.

A practice of meditation helps us to bear witness because that really is what meditation is. If you have an itch when you are meditating, you bear witness to the itch and don't scratch it. Then you observe how the itch goes away naturally without being scratched. If you have a thought about what to eat for breakfast or what you will say to a co-worker while you're meditating, you bear witness. You don't immediately act on it or chase the thought away. You watch it ebb, like a wave in the ocean, and flow back into the undefined mental space where it came from.

In our Western culture, we are hard-wired to respond to everything that happens to us, or around us, with either activity or speech. It sometimes seems impossible to de-program from that. Even in situations where there is absolutely nothing we can do, we still impulsively try to do or say something. Sometimes non-action is the smartest action. Sometimes not speaking is a better course than speaking.

In other words, ZIP IT!

As I have shared, I know how hard this path is. My speech is many times not right and my biggest problem is too much speech. It's difficult. That's why it's a practice, a very important practice. We stray from right speech all the time and we feel entirely justified in doing so because everyone else is talking the same way. The people in your world will support you in wrong speech. You will be enticed into wrong speech 100 times a day. And, if you try to keep to right speech, you won't find much support for your actions.

This practice will be difficult, but I promise to try harder if you do. And that means not just refraining from wrong speech but refraining from listening to wrong speech or approving of it, however tacitly. Listen to the speech around you from the people at lunch; on Facebook, Twitter, and all social media; TV and magazines. What do you hear? Is it true? Is it harsh? Is it divisive—even subtly? Is it gossip? Is it unnecessary? Are we speaking to help or are we speaking to pump up or defend our egos?

There are two sides to this practice: One side is keeping our speech right and the other side is not approving of untrue, harsh, idle speech, gossip, and divisive speech. How do we skillfully, gently, and compassionately disapprove of wrong speech without causing more divisiveness? The best way is not to engage. Say nothing.

It's human nature for people and even pets to continue behavior that gets the attention and generates the involvement of others. If the behavior is ignored by others, it is less likely to continue. If someone at work is raging in a divisive way about something, challenging or correcting their speech will only add energy to the communication and continue the negativity. Walking away without comment is like dumping a bucket of water on the flames. It may not stop the fire, but it won't intensify it.

This applies to social media, too. I recently posted a status on my Facebook timeline challenging myself and others not to like another's status if we don't agree or don't really like what the poster is commenting on, in a type of codependent social media behavior, which seems prevalent. It is the same if you don't like something. Just because Facebook offers an angry emoticon, it doesn't mean you have to use it. It might seem like common sense to challenge someone for a divisive post or divisive speech, in hopes you might help the speaker see the error of their ways, but it's not likely to change anything about the speaker's intent and resulting behavior and it is likely to cause conflict. It's a challenging practice!

I will close with a saying you've probably heard many times. There is much debate over who the author is. The Quote Investigator website believes this saying evolved over many decades:

> Let us be mindful of our **thoughts**, for they become our words;
> Our **words**, for they become our actions;
> Our **actions**, for they become **our habits;**
> Our **habits**, for they become our character;
> And our **character**, for it becomes our destiny.

There is an interesting mnemonic device you can take from this to help in your practice. Five of the keywords in the saying: words, actions, thoughts, character, and habits have initial letters that can spell the word "watch" if you switch the order around a bit. **WATCH is a great mantra to practice the whole of the Eightfold Path.**

Right Speech Practice: When to Speak; When to Listen

For the Right Speech practice tip, I suggest trying something inspired by what I've observed in myself and in those around me. As I've talked about in earlier sections, a combination of conditions that include social media and cable news, have created an openly divisive culture where we separate ourselves with political, religious, racial, sex, sexual preference, and economic labels that create "others" out of anyone who doesn't think like, look like, or believe like us.

Once those labels and boxes have divided us, we stop listening to each other. We believe we know that our side is right and everyone else is the "other" so they have nothing to say that we would want to hear. We get on social media and talk at each other rather than with each other, and we stop having dialogue with people who don't believe what we believe.

This environment that surrounds us supports reaction rather than wise action and reactive speaking rather than listening. How do we change the environment? As is the case with everything we've discussed up to this point, we first need to change ourselves. In the case of learning to listen, it starts with observing your behavior and your thoughts while in a conversation.

You can practice this by purposely focusing on a conversation with someone. You can choose someone you share the same views with first, then expand your practice to a conversation with someone who doesn't share your views. While in conversation notice when you have an urge to speak. Many times you will be speaking before you noticed that you had the urge to speak. That is reactive speaking. And reactive speaking tends to fill up the space where your conversation partner would feel invited to speak by your silence, by your active listening.

You will likely notice this reactive speaking habit to be more automatic and frequent when conversing with someone who doesn't share your views rather than the person who does. Yet, even when conversing with a person you are very comfortable with, you still might discover yourself jumping in to speak without stopping to notice if you thought about it first.

This is the practice. Be mindful of your urge to speak and ask yourself if what you are about to say adds to the conversation and is helpful. In other words, ask yourself if what you want to say is truthful, peaceful, gentle, and meaningful or if it's reactive.

Reflection on Right Speech

Many Colors of Water

Thinking of words I never spoke, I turn away from the path, stoop to hear a rock. It is much louder than the clamor of concealed expression—louder than its own polished image. Rocks talk in words not yet formed, singing the poetry of everything. Primordial language speaks what is without parenthetical distractions—how leaves are blue, the many colors of water, boundless emotion. I know you understand the dialect—it rushes from you in dreams while not in your own body, or as some spirit watcher. At morning, you surface from the flood of words knowing what you sound like, but not able to pronounce you again. Our stories live in these silent stanzas—I will let the rocks narrate me until you can hear without words.

~ Wendy Shinyo Haylett

-4-

RIGHT ACTION IS NOT REACTION

*"Do you have the patience to wait
till your mud settles and the water is clear?"*

— Lao Tzu, Tao Te Ching

IN READING THE VAST AMOUNT OF INFORMATION AVAILABLE ON THE INTERNET, in scholarly and modern books, and presentations on the Eightfold Path, I'm always bothered by the presentation of Right Action. Do you know what bothers me? The take-away from those new to Buddhism or sometimes for those not-so-new to Buddhism is that it's a focus on rules, things "not to do."

I don't know about you, but that's just the kind of thing that pushed me away from other religions and spiritual systems, bringing me to the study of Buddhism in the first place. I didn't want to hear about the things I was not supposed to do, so that I would be a good person, or get to heaven, or gain enlightenment, from some religious authority and then accept it at face value because they said so.

I started investigating Buddhism, like I imagine many of you did, to get away from pronouncements based on the words of humans passing along edicts supposedly received through personal connections with religious authorities or supernatural connections to supreme beings.

I don't believe that was the Buddha's intent. We can never really know, with certainty, the Buddha's intent, because his teachings were remembered and recorded by others in an oral tradition. But we do know that the Buddha taught by treating each person individually, according to their circumstances. This is what is meant by "skillful means" or *upaya*. A blanket set of rules for laypeople, everyday people, wouldn't make sense. Monks and nuns, yes, but not the others he taught. And part of his teachings was, "Don't take it on my authority alone. Test it yourself!"

My other complaint about the more typical presentations of Right Action is that Right View is not emphasized. Right Intention is, most of the time, but the concept of the why behind the action seems to disappear and break the natural wholeness of the Eightfold Path. As I've written earlier, despite the reference to a path, it isn't a step-by-step process. It is not a linear list, but a circle: a holistic system designed for the strength of all the components together.

In your Dharma journey, you will learn more and more about what right view is, causing you to discard outdated concepts and worldviews, then that will cause you to modify your intentions, and hopefully, discard old habits, negative thinking, speaking, and action. This is the underlying wholeness of the path taught by The Buddha. The Eightfold Path is a spiritual organism. As you practice, the organic wholeness becomes easier to understand. At first, all the lists, numbers, and steps seem like commandments to memorize and adhere to—that is until you reflect, meditate, and practice—then the fundamental interdependence begins to slowly come into focus.

Commitment to the discipline of the path follows as a natural consequence of understanding. A confidence that you could refer to as faith follows understanding and drives your practice. The unique quality of the Buddhist path is that it flows from logic and basic understanding, as the grounds for practice rather than the opposite. Typically, when you think of faith, you think of belief in something you have no direct knowledge of or experience with. As a blind acceptance. The Buddhist path is underpinned by direct experience and confidence in the effectiveness of the practice. This is the faith of Buddhism.

So, in the beginning, there is an idea. The seed from which all else germinates. The view we hold of the world will dictate the course of our actions. The path of Right View begins with an understanding of the basic facts of our existence, **The Four Noble Truths, which I will review again here but can also be found in Part 5:**

1. **To be alive and not enlightened is to experience dissatisfaction.**

2. **This dissatisfaction is borne of attachment, craving, or grasping.** If we like something, someone, or some experience, we want to keep it forever without anything changing. This stems from an ignorance about the nature of reality and the nature of what really makes us happy.

3. **This habit of craving and grasping—the stickiness of the mind—can be stopped.** Our dissatisfaction or suffering over not getting what we want, getting what we don't want, and about things changing, can be extinguished. Things change and are impermanent. That won't change. However, our dissatisfaction or suffering over change and impermanence can change.

4. **The way we can extinguish this and not experience dissatisfaction is through practicing the Eightfold Path.** The Buddha taught that we can rid ourselves of this dissatisfaction because he did it first, then he taught us how to do it.

The Second Arrow: Acceptance IS Action

Suffering is an experience all living things share. Two people may experience an identical illness or injury causing an identical level of pain, if it could be measured. The pain of the original illness or injury can be referred to as the first arrow. One person may accept it gracefully and find ways to experience it, live it fully. and make the best of it. Another will suffer a psychological hell of their own making and their experience of that hell is much worse than the pain and discomfort of the injury or illness.

The essential difference between the experience of two people sharing an identical misfortune is due to the excessive desire of one, versus the acceptance of the other. The source of their problems lies not in the actual experience of injury or illness, but in their view of it and their reaction to it. They created the bulk of their suffering. They shot themselves with a "second arrow."

The Buddha explained this in the *Sallatha Sutta*:

> *When touched with a feeling of pain, the uninstructed run-of-the-mill person sorrows, grieves, and laments, beats his breast, becomes distraught. So he feels two pains, physical and mental. Just as if they were to shoot a man with an arrow and, right afterward, were to shoot him with another one, so that he would feel the pains of two arrows....*

Now, the well-instructed disciple of the noble ones, when touched with a feeling of pain, does not sorrow, grieve, or lament, does not beat his breast or become distraught. So he feels one pain: physical, but not mental. Just as if they were to shoot a man with an arrow and, right afterward, did not shoot him with another one, so that he would feel the pain of only one arrow....

As he (the well-instructed disciple) is touched by that painful feeling, he is not resistant. No resistance-obsession with regard to that painful feeling obsesses him. Touched by that painful feeling, he does not delight in sensual pleasure.... He is disjoined, I tell you, from suffering and stress.

~Arrow Sutra, from Access to Insight

It seems ridiculous, doesn't it? Shooting ourselves with a second arrow. But we do it all the time, don't we? We double-down on any little crappy thing that happens to us. And it seems to me that we double-down more readily on the little crappy things than the BIG ones, like catastrophic illness, misfortunate, or loss. We have a way of tormenting ourselves over the littlest of disappointments.

Yet, if we did as the Buddha said of the well-instructed disciple, we would understand that it is in our clinging to feeling good and clinging to comfort that causes the second arrow. How dare life interfere with our comfort and our need to have things just right?! Yet that's not how life works. Things happen according to causes and conditions: mine, yours, the weather, ice on the driveway, the car, viruses, a miserable boss. This is what renunciation means.

As I've mentioned before, renunciation in Tibetan means "authentic becoming." It does not necessarily mean living in isolation from the world, but a renouncing of the delusions that keep us from becoming our authentic selves, flexibly living life as it presents itself, not as we would like life to be.

It means giving up clinging to the appearance of things as something, someone out there happening to us. It means, instead of grasping tightly to the things that will only cause suffering and clinging desperately to things as we would like them to be, we accept or surrender to things exactly as they are.

Imagine you are a tree in the wind. In all but the most severe windstorms, trees sway and bend with the wind. They go along for the ride and when the wind is over, they are still standing. They are the same trees. You don't hear them muttering, complaining, or crying out, feeling sorry for themselves that the wind is interfering with their otherwise perfect day. You may hear the snapping of small branches, but no major groaning.

Most of us in the west today view this sort of flexibility or acceptance as a kind of moral cowardice. Caught up in frustration over our first-world problems, like slow Internet speed or an incorrect take-out order, our needs and ultimate comfort are our primary concerns. It's as if the words of Dylan Thomas about death as defeat, "Do not go gentle into that good night, but rage; rage against the dying of the light" has become our anthem about anything that happens as a challenge to what we want when we want it.

But the truth is, acceptance is not a passive state, desire is. This is one of the misunderstandings inherent in our modern world view. Acceptance is a conscious awareness of the reality of one's situation and does not imply a lack of action or positive energy. Acceptance is action because it deals with things as they are, with suchness. Attachment to desire is a type of frenetic non-action that ignores reality in favor of a dream or illusion. The illusion that to be happy we must always be comfortable. There are too many examples of happy people living with physical and emotional challenges or living in seemingly unbearable environmental conditions, like extreme heat or extreme cold, to believe that our illusion of comfort as the cause of happiness is based on the facts of reality, things as they are.

Understanding and accepting reality is the beginning of enlightened action. In order to pursue a goal, we must have a grasp of what the conditions are that will shape the direction of our efforts or actions. The power of this teaching arises directly from its unconditioned freedom. But this freedom can only be obtained when we have the courage to pioneer into the self with our eyes open.

Remembering Interdependence: Preventing Reaction

According to Buddhist teachings, the fundamental reality of the universe is the "Buddha Mind" and that is none other than our own original nature. This nature is hidden from us through our desires and attachments, which are habits of lifetimes. This is the ignorance that blocks our authentic becoming. We have an attachment to an elusive dream self that keeps us from seeing our true nature. We are literally unable to see the forest for all the trees, and yet there is no forest other than all these trees.

The result of practicing the Eightfold Path is to begin to see each tree or thing for what it is, a perfect expression of time and space. Every tree in the forest is a mirror to the process of becoming, and the forest, too, is becoming. All of life becomes merged in mutual identity at this subtle level of understanding. This is the result of a change of perspective that allows a perception of reality as a dynamic whole, rather than a set of discrete structures in a linear, causal relationship.

When we see a tree, we usually identify it by a type, like maple or oak. That is a linear perspective that ignores the tree's interaction with the rest of the environment. A tree is a dynamic process, rather than a concrete unit of being. An oak tree was an acorn, after all. It's a process. Yet we perceive it as a discrete thing, a tree, because of the limits imposed on our senses and the corresponding interpretation by our mind.

Our eyes perceive light reflected from a source within the limits imposed by the visible spectrum. Although we are aware of the science demonstrating other radiations, like infrared and ultraviolet light, we are unable to perceive it. Though the energy of light is composed of undulating patterns or waves, our perception of change is limited, and we are unable to see these different forms and changes in energy. Yet, we can see these changes when we look at a time-lapse film of a garden flower or the acorn becoming an oak tree.

The Buddhist term "mutual interpenetration" or "interdependence" recognizes this dynamic interplay. Every aspect of the garden is affecting and being affected by all other aspects simultaneously. The sun, the wind, rain or no rain, insects, and birds aerating the soil and dropping seeds. The evidence of this reality is recognized in many disciplines from ecology to particle physics. The essential point, from a Buddhist perspective, is that our own being is also sharing in this interpenetration!

There is no inherent reality of self, outside of this interpenetration. No permanent soul, mind, or spirit that is not one with this eternal interchange. The process is being, there is nothing else. The forest is the tree and the trees are the forest. The rose is the garden, and the garden, the rose. Others are the self, and self is the other. There is nothing other than this, nothing to cling to and nothing to fear. For if all is self, then there is no self which can be threatened by another.

Understanding and accepting reality—seeing life as it is, rather than as you would like it to be—is the beginning of enlightened activity. The process of thought cannot be separated from the process of intention and will. There is constant interaction. This is important for us to remember because it forces us to recognize how our actions affect our world view. It is simple to see how our viewpoint affects our actions because in most cases our actions are predicated upon a conscious view.

What we may not see is that whenever we choose to act, that action, in turn, affects our view of the world. The action we take is registered in our unconscious as memory and then becomes available as a reference for future actions. Every time we face a situation that calls for action, we are required to analyze the situation through the cognitive process and then make a choice, activating the will. In the process, we are accessing our memory, and our memory contains both the memory of our previous actions and our worldview as well. This begins a process where the mind searches for continuity or conformity between the past action and worldview.

Memory links pertinent data together in order to give our conscious mind a pattern of information appropriate to the situation. If our actions are not consistent with our worldview, it creates a problem for the unconscious. How does it know what information to provide us with if there aren't natural patterns of consistency? Our unconscious is left with only two choices: it can ignore our worldview and access memories consistent with our past actions, or relegate views held—but not acted upon—to a kind of subdirectory.

The mind balks at this kind of conflict and reacts to the inherent tension between worldview and the actions taken that are inconsistent with our worldview. In other words, every time we take an action that violates what we know to be right, it causes chaos in our unconscious. What eventually develops is either a great deal of emotional turmoil or a duplicitous spiritual character that is habitual.

That is why establishing a robust worldview that is strong enough to power intention is so important. That is why taking some time each day—five, fifteen, 20 or 30 minutes, preferably two times each day—to reflect and meditate on how your worldview and understanding of what is right or is not right is consistent with your actions.

When you consciously try to build mindfulness into your day, what you notice is that sometimes not speaking and not acting is the best possible action, the Right Action. Our action-oriented (and reaction-oriented!) culture has hard-wired us to respond to everything that happens to us, or around us, with either activity or speech. It is nearly impossible to de-program. Even in situations where there is absolutely nothing we can do, we still impulsively try to do or say something. Many times, though, non-action is the smartest action, as Lao Tzu taught about waiting until the mud has settled.

The truth is, we often react without thinking. It's a gut reaction, often based on fear and insecurities. Responding, on the other hand, is taking the situation in and deciding the best course of action based on values such as reason, compassion, and cooperation. For example:

React: Your child breaks something. You immediately react by getting angry, perhaps yelling, upsetting the child and yourself, worsening your relationship, not making anything better.

Respond: Your child breaks something. You notice your anger reaction, but you pause, take a breath and consider the situation. Your first response is to see if your child is OK. Is she hurt, scared? Second, realize that the object that is broken, in the larger view, is not that important. Let it go, adjust your expectations. Third, help her clean up, make a game of it, show her that mistakes happen and that it's not something to dwell on. Fourth, calmly talk about how to avoid mistakes like that in the future and give her a hug.

This choice presents itself to us all the time, whether it's our mother nagging us, our co-worker being rude, our husband not being kind enough, and so on. There will always be external events that bother us, but if we learn to respond and not just react, we can make things better and not worse.

The main thing to learn is mindfulness and the pause. Mindfulness means watching ourselves when something happens that might normally upset us or trigger an emotional reaction. Pay close attention to how your mind reacts. Then pause. You don't have to act immediately, just because you have an internal reaction. We can pause, not act, breathe. We can watch the urge to act irrationally arise, then watch it go away. Sometimes that takes a few seconds, other times it means we should remove ourselves politely from the situation and let ourselves cool down before we respond.

Pause. Watch the reaction go away.

The Five Precepts: Gentle Guides, Not Commandments

We can't look at Right Action without looking at the rules of The Five Precepts and The Ten Freedom Vows. Ah, rules. In Buddhism? Buddhism is not easy to classify, despite people trying to put it into a box, which is the perfect illustration of what Buddhism teaches. Nothing or no one can be put into a box, caught and classified as one thing or another. Because we aren't—and nothing is—any one, discrete thing.

Some people come to Buddhism looking for religion. Others come to it as an escape from another religion yet offering some sort of cogent world view and/or spiritual practice. And others are attracted to it because of the meditative aspect and a desire to "bliss out" or reach a state of enlightenment that will free them from all their troubles. If you come to Buddhism as a religion, you might expect rules. If you come to Buddhism as an escape from religion or for the meditative aspect, then rules would be a turn-off.

My impetus propelling me into Buddhism was a combination of all of those. I had 'almost' found the faith my mother had in God, during my pre-teen and early teen years. But, as is the case many times, my teen years were marked by an intellectual rebellion against most things my mother, father, or society in general held dear.

I first started reading about Buddhism in my teens, starting with Siddhartha by Herman Hesse. I dug deeper with Alan Watts, Philip Kapleau, and Shunryu Suzuki, then I explored Hinduism, the *Upanishads*, and the *Bhagavad Gita*, and spent a little time talking to the Hari Krishna folks and chanting because of George Harrison's influence.

During my teens and early twenties, I fought panic attacks and a profound fear of death. It first visited me when I was younger, then reemerged in my late teens. So, during that time, my spiritual searching was driven by an urge for comfort and help through anxieties and fears. I was looking for a transcendent comforter (God, Krishna, Jesus) to hold on to and get me through my fears.

I fell away from the grasping for a comforter, as my panic attacks and anxieties eased through work with a psychiatrist specializing in anxiety, and then through throwing myself into my work. When I did come back to Buddhism, I was driven by a psychological and philosophical curiosity. But there was always a part of me looking for the faith I almost grasped as a child and the transcendent comforter I searched for in my teens and twenties.

Buddhism, with its seeming calm and meditative approach, and its philosophical and psychological heft, offered all the things I was looking for. And the best part was that no matter how much I investigated, there were always more and different paths to explore. So, if one wasn't cutting it for me, I looked deeper into another. Starting with Zen, then going deep into Tibetan Buddhist studies in the Gelugpa school with Geshe teachers, then practicing with a Drikung Kagyu sangha and visiting Rinpoches and Khenpos, until I found a home with the Bright Dawn Center of Oneness Buddhism, and a personal spiritual centering place made up of all I studied and practiced, but with a primary Shin and Zen view.

And through it all, I know for sure I was not looking for some new set of moral guidelines. I was already pretty uptight, as I indicated earlier, and tended to cling to traditional things when insecure. So, what I think I saw in Buddhism was a path that would loosen me up and "chill" me out yet offer the peace of something to believe in or a "big story" to commit myself to.

From that background, I have consistently had an uneasy relationship with the precepts and vows as admonishments. My personal experience with them—and the experience I witnessed with others' relationships with the precepts—was that they produce far more questions than they answer. Clinging to the Five Precepts as rules, laws, or edicts of moral authority coming from the Buddha can cause more suffering than it prevents, in some instances.

When you look at the precepts from a fundamental surface view, most seem impossible to keep. Like not killing. No matter what we do, even just sleeping, we are killing bugs. The Buddha was aware of all the bugs and worms being killed, as he was watching farmland being tilled. Walking across your yard will surely result in the death of beetles, ants, worms, and maybe even a small toad.

And what about lying? Circling back to our earlier discussion on Right Speech in relationship to social media, am I lying if I "like" a post of a friend's new profile picture when I don't really think the picture is that flattering of him?

This is part of my unease around the precepts. For people in the "real world", the precepts can be useful if they can be skillfully incorporated as guidelines for practice, but they can also be mistakenly seen as rigid commandments or moral absolutes. The precepts should be a framework of questioning that turns us away from ourselves and toward how we can serve others rather than a set of rules that make us feel like failures.

When they become another set of rules and "thou shalls" they build barriers to questioning, meditating, and understanding the Dharma and Right View, as I believe the Buddha intended.

Clinging rigidly to what we believe or the "right" rules or "right" behavior can separate people from each other—as if we need any more of that in today's world—and can separate individuals from embracing and gaining a deeper understanding of their own mind and the Dharma, especially if they feel like failures.

I am sure we've all had the experience, directly or indirectly, of being involved in a passionate or heated discussion, on-line or in-person, about veganism or vegetarianism versus meat-eating—among Buddhists and non-Buddhists alike. But when it happens in a virtual or real-life Buddhist community, it does little to help anyone, nor does it generally change minds. What it does do is create a tighter grip on opinions and judgments or make new practitioners feel like they either don't belong or that they are failures.

How can that help anyone? How does that relieve suffering?

The precepts should be used as training wheels, helpful when we are just finding our balance, but later they can be a cumbersome interference to moment-to-moment, on-the-ground wisdom.

In my experience, the moment-to-moment, on-the-ground wisdom is the ticket to using the precepts skillfully. And that takes the working of the Eightfold Path, especially Right View and Right Intention, applied in a meditative effort to understand how to work with the Precepts. This represents the problem I have with the precepts as something to focus on in beginning Buddhism or Everyday Buddhism. Beginning Buddhist practitioners, or those who want to adopt the guidelines and practices to their everyday lives, need to understand the Four Noble Truths and practice the Eightfold Path to reinforce that understanding until it becomes their own thinking, their own perspective. Without that, Right Understanding can never result, and the precepts then represent empty words and external rules.

A fundamentalist attitude is never skillful in Buddhist practice. Too often, people confuse the Five Precepts with a rigid system of ethics they must follow, even before they have a basic understanding of the Four Noble Truths or the Eightfold Path. We know from the Buddha's teachings of the Four Noble Truths that the reason we feel dissatisfaction is because of grasping and craving. And we also know that the Buddha promised a way out—freedom from that grasping—through the practice of the Eightfold Path.

Some grasp to the precepts, thinking it is the obedience to them that will set them free. There is some truth to that. The precepts offer a path that can condition the mind and body so that you have created a clear vehicle for meditation and right view. The purpose is as a mental training regimen that will gradually rid your mind of upset or disturbance.

We can be weak people, for sure. I will speak for myself here and say that I do sometimes give in to cravings for experiences or things that aren't the best for keeping mental discipline. For those who have trouble disciplining their minds and their behavior, the precepts are good functional training wheels that can help break bad habits.

They can work on a subtle level where, in the process of avoiding unskillful behaviors, we rearrange how we think about and react to certain situations. Once we begin to avoid being led by desires, we will find new ways to deal with our desires and feelings. And in those new ways, we will be free from habitual grasping.

Many times, we are caught in what one of my teachers called a "klesha attack." A klesha is the Sanskrit word referring to mental states that cloud the mind and manifest in unwholesome actions like anxiety, fear, anger, jealousy, desire, depression, etc. If used as tools and not as weapons of judgment (of ourselves or others) or divisiveness, then I embrace the teaching and practice of the precepts. If they are thought of as a kind mother protecting me from my own blind or ignorant passions, the precepts are skillful.

Understanding Various Approaches to the Five Precepts

Theravada

The Theravada tradition uses the Five Precepts as a model of restraint. Restraining from certain activities helps develop a peaceful mind. The Buddha said, "not to commit evil but to practice all good and to keep the heart pure." If we keep our hearts pure does not mean pure as in being a saint but being aware of our own thoughts and activities so that we can be open to others. So that we can approach our lives in an open, compassionate way—compassion that extends to others and our self—not clouded by the poisons of hatred, greed, or delusion.

Mahayana

The Mahayana Buddhist philosophy of emptiness or sunyata teaches that every person, act, and object (all things) are empty of intrinsic existence and nature. Therefore, nothing can be inherently bad or good. Everything depends on intention and circumstances or as my Sensei, Rev. Koyo Kubose teaches, everything depends on person, place, and time.

Vajrayana / Tibetan

The Vajrayana uses both the negative aspects of life and the positive aspects as tools for transformation, so the Five Precepts, although relevant, can also be thought of as focuses for practice.

It's best to look at all three approaches as complementary. Sometimes it is better to practice restraint, other times we should look deeper—beyond categorizations of right, wrong, good, or bad and do what's best, or skillful, based on the specific situation presenting using the person, place, and time perspective. Other times doing nothing externally is best, instead, sit in reflection of our thought and actions so that we might be able to transform them from within.

The typical presentation of the Five Precepts: Do Not Do:

1. **Do not kill** (refrain from destroying living creatures).

2. **Do not steal** (refrain from taking what is not given).

3. **Do not misuse sex** (refrain from sexual misconduct).

4. **Do not lie** (refrain from incorrect speech).

5. **Do not indulge in intoxicants** (refrain from substances leading to carelessness)

Let's look at them from an "Everyday Buddhism" perspective, as gentle guides, not commandments. It is more inspiring to state the precepts positively. And they can be even more effective if you reword or rework them in a way that would address your own intentions or help you work with issues in your own life. I've reworded them in a positive presentation of the Five Precepts.

The "Everyday Buddhism" Approach to the Five Precepts: Do

1. **I will protect and support life and strive to love and understand others.**

   The First Precept is to protect and support life and strive to love and understand others. This precept can raise major hot-button issues, from veganism to abortion, euthanasia, capital punishment, serving in the military, to medical research. I've had podcast listeners reach out to me with concerns about their actions regarding this precept. These issues can be the cause of judgment and divisiveness.

I've discussed this before, but it bears repeating that every Buddhist school, lineage, and teacher interprets the precepts differently. Theravada Buddhists say that a violation of the first precepts involves five factors: First, there is a living being. Second, there is the perception that the being is a living being. Third, there is the conscious chosen thought of killing. Fourth, the killing is carried out. Fifth, the being dies.

This teaching indicates that there must be a willful thought of killing that being to violate the precept. And this includes having someone else do the actual killing. And according to this teaching, a premeditated killing is a graver offense than a killing that is impulsive, such as in self-defense.

In Mahayana teachings, the first precept is explained from the perspective of nurturing the mind to protect all beings. This from the *Mahayana Brahajala* or *Brahma Net Sutra*:

A disciple of the Buddha shall not himself kill, encourage others to kill, kill by expedient means, praise killing, rejoice at witnessing killing, or kill through incantation or deviant mantras. He must not create the causes, conditions, methods, or karma of killing, and shall not intentionally kill any living creature. As a Buddha's disciple, he ought to nurture a mind of compassion... always devising expedient means to rescue and protect all beings. If instead, he fails to restrain himself and kills sentient beings without mercy, he commits a major offense.

The precepts approach slippery subjects and shouldn't be viewed as absolutes. If it is necessary to kill one person to save many others, then that is not a violation of the injunction against killing, but an expression of the spirit behind the injunction. As absolutes, they can cause misinterpretation, miscommunication, confusion, and disputes about major cultural issues or hot-button topics, as I mentioned earlier.

Let's look at some of these issues, starting with eating meat. People often associate Buddhism with vegetarianism. Although most schools of Buddhism encourage vegetarianism, it is generally considered a personal choice, not a requirement. From the sutras, it is clear the historical Buddha was not a strict vegetarian. The first monks obtained all their food by begging, and the Buddha taught his monks to eat whatever food they were given, including meat. However, if a monk knew an animal had been slaughtered specifically to feed monks, the meat was to be refused.

Then there is Buddhism and euthanasia, which is something one of my podcast listeners wrote about in relation to medical testing. I've read or heard teachers say that Buddhism does not support euthanasia. But, again, there doesn't seem to be anything I can find that would point to a hard-and-fast rule against euthanasia. A prominent Zen teacher says it is selfish not to euthanize a suffering animal out of personal squeamishness. If we remember that easing our own suffering through the practice of the Eightfold Path is what the Buddha taught and Mahayana Buddhist teachings elaborated on this teaching with the path of the Bodhisattva, then the suffering of all beings is our concern.

Buddhism and military service is another topic a listener wrote to me about. There are thousands of Buddhists serving in the U.S. armed forces, including some Buddhist chaplains. Buddhism does not demand absolute pacifism, but it does show how countries can be caught in the same grasping trap of greed, hatred, and ignorance as individuals are. So, war is something that should cause pause and consideration, in the same way as we meditate on anger.

If we use the traditional words of the First Precept of "do not kill" it is a vow that is literally impossible to maintain. We all kill every day. That is not to say we are all killers. It is not our intention to kill but destroying other creatures or contributing to killing in some way is unavoidable. We eat food and wear clothing that in the process of their production can involve taking the lives of animals. We kill insects and rodents to prevent the spreading of disease. And, as I mentioned earlier, even walking across our own yards can result in the killing of insects and other small creatures.

This type of killing is unintentional. We can make personal choices that will minimize killing resulting from activities we engage in and to help protect the lives of other beings. These choices call on the Mahayana view of relating to the precepts. An understanding that everything depends on intention and circumstances and an understanding of a broader view of protecting and supporting life. This is especially true of questions related to abortion, life support, elective suicide, euthanasia, and scientific or medical research.

There is always a bigger picture or greater good that our own opinions and prejudices can prevent us from seeing. An understanding of sunyata helps frame these questions using both compassion and wisdom to rise above our own small perspective of what is good or bad, right or wrong. Many times I have witnessed passionate and heated discussions centering around the tricky questions of vegetarianism, abortion, euthanasia, and research where each side of the argument is convinced that their view is right and right for everyone. Yet we know from the teaching of *sunyata* that nothing or no single way of being can be inherently bad or good.

Opinions about these things are just opinions. And in this Internet world, we can collect and spew multiple sources of others' opinions to use of proof of our rightness. Think for yourself. Decide for yourself. But don't decide for others unless you have determined through compassionate consideration that your suggestion for another would help protect and support their life. And remember if they don't agree with you, it is their choice. And their choice is not wrong. It's always a matter of person, place, and time.

There are other ways we can honor the First Precept through our speech and actions. A harsh comment could kill years of trust or a snide remark could kill another's inspiration. In taking another person for granted we could kill a relationship. This kind of killing falls within our rewording of the First Precept of striving to love and understand others.

2. **I will take only what is freely given and practice gratitude and generosity.**

The second precept is harder than it seems. We all know not to grab a piece of fruit at the grocery store without paying for it or taking a pen from your friend's desk because you like it. But are you breaking the precept when you use work time for looking at Facebook or ordering something from Amazon? When you use your roommate's shampoo without asking? Or when you take pens home from work? Or how about when you exaggerate your tax deductions?

This precept, like all of them, should be used as reflections or meditations on your behavior, your motivation, and the results. Why did you do what you did? And did it cause any harm to yourself or others?

In addition to not taking what isn't freely given, the second precept encourages the practice of gratitude and generosity. As you go through your day, watch to see what ways you are giving and taking. Are you taking, or being given, more than you are giving? Look at all your interactions, even the smallest ones. Did you wipe up your coffee spill on the counter? That is giving cleanliness and order to your living companions and it is an act of generosity. Did you offer to get your co-worker or spouse a cup of coffee when you walked by? In what little ways might you strengthen your generosity?

You can also monitor your actions from an inner perspective by looking at ways you grasp or want things. Consider your own greed, no matter how subtle. Excessively looking out for own comfort is an example of subtle greed. Those of us living a comfortable existence cling to comfort. We want more and more of it. We are irritated when it's too hot, too cold, or too noisy.

If we really look at how and what we grasp or crave, it's easy to see how tenuous our connection is to generosity, moderation, and sense of inner contentment. Greed and grasping are rooted in delusion, the misconception that our well-being depends on acquiring a certain object, experience, or relationship. With practice, we can begin to see that our being ... our aliveness ... our awareness is enough.

It's funny, isn't it? We clamor for a simpler life, yet every minute we are presented with the opportunity to not want something else. To rest in the moment is being enough. Try being attentive to moments when you desire something strongly. This feeling is typically colored by self-centeredness, a lack of connection to others, a feeling of being out of balance or out of control, an obliviousness to consequences, and even a sense of entitlement.

Another way to look at the second precept is to expand our reflection beyond individual behavior to broader cultural and social ethics. Do we participate in any activity that harms others or prevents others from obtaining fair financial reimbursement for their work? We may not have stolen anything from anyone in our entire lives but the culture we participate in may be contributing to something that amounts to stealing. And if we are living a relatively comfortable Western lifestyle, then we participate in a culture driven by the engine of buying and selling.

I don't wish to begin a critique of the capitalist system and I'm not implying that you or I directly deprive others or contribute to the suffering of others, yet the constant backbeat in our current culture screams "buy this!" Greed and grasping are the very tendencies that marketing people energize in us. Commercials on TV and ads in our Facebook and Twitter feeds reinforce wanting and our sense of entitlement. The stronger our sense of entitlement becomes the weaker our ability to see our own tendency to greed and grasping.

These tendencies are deeply ingrained in our broader social and cultural way of being. And we have internalized them so much that we are oblivious to our own sense of entitlement. We are conditioned to expect a certain type of food, house or apartment to live in, car to drive, smartphone to use, job and pay to expect. Why me and not another? Can we try to see how it touches every area of our life in our everyday choices of food, clothing, driving, relaxing, being in nature, and investing? What is our own personal relationship to what can be seen as a social privilege?

3. **I will respect and support on-going relationships, honor my commitments, and practice discernment in sexual activity without compulsiveness.**

I doubt that anyone reading this book would approach this precept with a fundamentalist view toward sexual and gender identity or non-traditional relationships, so I won't even touch on those issues.

As is the case with all the precepts, these are not rules. This precept is about acting from our intimate connection to another, without harm or disrespect. Breaking the precept through sexual misconduct would be any act that causes harm to someone, like infidelity. But this precept also touches on craving and clinging by avoiding attachment to the senses. Can we find a quality in our sexual feelings that is not clinging and attachment, but a more profound and joyful, appreciative relatedness?

What about restraint? For those who have sexual addiction issues, it is not a question of "just saying no," or abstinence. It is a question of gaining insight into our motives and drives to generate a feeling of corresponding responsibility for our actions. Once we have realized our true intentions, we can make mindful choices that enable us to enjoy our sexuality, compassionately and mindfully.

No rules can help us if we feel controlled by unconscious forces, and that is where the true spirit of the third precept can help us. The third precept counsels us to maintain awareness, to know ourselves deeply, to be aware of what is happening at the moment, and to extend that awareness to those around us, fully realizing our interconnection.

4. **I will say what is true, useful, and timely, and practice deep listening so that my speaking and listening reflects loving-kindness and compassion.**

Right speech is a big deal in Buddhism. It's the fourth precept and the third step on the Eightfold Path. Yes, it's about telling the truth but it's also about using speech to share love and joy, and not injure.

I previously mentioned deep listening in the section on right speech, but I will admit that this is something I work with a lot. That means I fail, but I keep trying. It is about being more aware of the other and what they are saying than thinking about what you want to say or expressing your point of view. Without deep listening, loving speech is not possible. We have to listen in order to understand what's going on in another's mind and heart. Their worries ... their desires ... their suffering. Once we have understood, we can help them with compassion. And sometimes that means to keep quiet and just be a listener. Just be someone who they can count on to listen.

We need to listen to ourselves to know what's really going on inside. Listening to and knowing what we're thinking and what we're feeling prevents us from reacting to what's going on externally. We need to learn to listen deeply to our partner and family. Right speech prompts us to ask our loved ones: "What could I do to make you happier?" and then to listen to the reply without judging or reacting. Right speech prompts us to say, "Thank you for being here for me. Your presence enriches my life. Please tell me how I can love you better."

There are some sticky questions people wonder about when reflecting on right speech. One of them is, "Is it okay to tell a white lie?" We've all been there. Sometimes the truth is too hurtful. So, it depends very much on how you tell the truth. However, in Buddhism, we never say that certain conduct is "right" or "wrong." It is not possible to give blueprints for ethical behavior because every situation is different.

If you are wondering whether or not you should tell the truth, you should examine your motivation very carefully. Then ask others what they think because they may see the situation more clearly than you can.

An everyday example of a lie inspired by a motivation to help—in other words, a white lie—is when a friend asks you if you like her new haircut and you don't but respond that you do. How someone's hair looks changes every day. It's very possible that you would like her haircut better tomorrow. And it's entirely possible that everyone else but you might love her haircut. There is no reason to be honest in this situation. An honest "no" answer could cause your friend to feel insecure for the day or longer. That would cause you friend to suffer.

An example of a lie that some people might consider a white lie is a quick brush-off or ignoring a tough conversation that should be initiated because you are too uncomfortable, too busy, or too insecure. Suppose your friend was rude to a waitress while you were at lunch and the waitress expressed her hurt and anger by not being attentive through the rest of the meal. On your way home from lunch, your friend asks, "What was wrong with that waitress? Why did she rush us through our meal? Did we do something wrong?" Some people might let this go to avoid an uncomfortable situation with your friend.

The precept is to say what is true, useful, and timely, and practice deep listening so that our speaking and listening reflects loving-kindness and compassion. There is a lot to that positive expression of not lying. Let's look at each component through this situation with your friend and the waitress.

The truth is that your friend was rude to the waitress. Is it useful to tell him so? It might be, depending on your friend's pattern of behavior. Does he act rude or thoughtlessly with others when he is under stress? Does he have a habit of thinking everyone else is acting badly without considering his own behavior? Is it timely?

If you have time to have a good conversation then that would be the time. If you both have to rush back to work, suggest that you talk more about it after work. And in practicing deep listening, you can almost hear your friend asking to have his behavior checked when he asks, "Did we do something wrong?" Does telling him that he was rude express loving-kindness and compassion. Yes, it might hurt him at first. It might even cause him to be angry with you. But if you gently mention to him, without a tone of judgment, that it appeared to you that he acted rudely to the waitress so it may have appeared that way to her, too. Then your intention is compassion for both your friend, the waitress, and any waitress or another person he may act that way in the future.

Another question that sometimes comes up is: "When and how is it inappropriate to express our anger?" The key—and this is difficult—is to try not to express anger when you are in the grips of it! When anger is in control of you, your mind is clouded, and you will most likely regret whatever you say. Take a few moments to focus on your breath and nothing else. This will clear your mind. When you are calm and in control of your mind, then you can open a dialogue.

And another frequent question is, "Is it okay to gossip?" Generally, I would say, "No." I think the best rule of thumb is to not say anything about anyone when they're not present that you wouldn't say if they were standing in front of you. Social media has blurred that line. Today we say a lot of things virtually. So much so, as I mentioned earlier in reference to "The Online Disinhibition Effect" studied by sociologists, we may say something online that we would never consider saying face-to-face. The invisibility of online messaging and texting gives people a sense of inhibition and tempts them to say things that they otherwise wouldn't. Too often I witness people saying things on social media and texting stuff about another that I'm pretty sure they wouldn't say to anyone in person.

And, because of this, watching how you respond internally to things you read and hear on social media is a great training ground for the practice of right speech. Question yourself before saying, typing, or texting anything.

5. **I will maintain a clear and alert mind that is aware of its motivations, moment-to-moment so that I can discern between what is the cause of suffering and what is not the cause of suffering.**

This precept opens the door to as many grey areas and hot-button issues as the first precept. Worded positively it is: I will maintain a clear and alert mind that is aware of its motivations, moment-to-moment so that I can discern between what is the cause of suffering and what is not the cause of suffering.

The essence of this precept is that we need to avoid anything that leads us to behave without being mindful. It means thinking about whether we're doing something as an escape or way to deal with restlessness, anxiety, and pain.

Traditionally, this precept of no intoxicants is understood as not using addictive substances. Many things, not just alcohol or drugs, can be used in such a way that they become intoxicants: coffee, tea, chewing gum, sweets, sex, sleep, TV, social media, video games, power, fame.

If you're proud of being abstinent from everything listed by name in the old rules, while still engaging in compulsive and addictive Facebooking and video game playing, then you have completely missed the point of the precepts themselves.

It is true, of course, that alcohol and other intoxicating substances are more likely to lead to indulgence and loss of clarity. For this reason, a rule of thumb that says "no intoxicating substances" is pretty good, as rules go. But anyone who is more interested in following rules to the letter than they are in truly understanding how their own mind works and how it relates to real experience is not going to get very far in Buddhist practice.

When we don't fully experience life as it is manifesting itself in the present moment, we become possessed by craving. In a state of craving, we may want to bring something else into our experience to make us more alert, to loosen or calm us, to sharpen the mind and body or dull it, or to give us pleasure or take away pain. This explains how suffering is created. Suffering is created from ignorance, craving, and aversion.

We can try to reduce the craving for things like intoxicating substances or anything or activity that dulls the present moment or heightens the present moment, depending on whether we're grasping at the present or wishing it would go away (aversion). But without understanding *that* we're grasping at or pushing something away, and without understanding *why* we are doing so, we are less likely to stop the pattern completely. The starting point then is to clear up our ignorance about what is going on in our minds.

Clearing up ignorance is the only true way to alleviate suffering. And that can only happen by looking at our own minds. Looking at the precepts as rules of ethics about seeking permission to do something and looking for someone or something to tell us we can't do something. This permission seeking assumes there is someone or something else in authority—society, or perhaps God—who will reward or punish us for breaking the rules.

When we work with precepts, we should do so with the understanding that "self" and "other" are delusions. This concept of ethics is not one based on a transactional experience. It is firmly anchored in the non-dual perspective central to Buddhist philosophy.

There is nothing external to us acting as an authority. This requires working with ourselves on a very deep and intimate level, honestly evaluating our own motivations and thinking deeply about how our actions will affect others. And by doing this, we will open ourselves to wisdom and compassion, to an enlightened vision and enlightened activities.

The Freedom Vows: Right Action Guidelines

There are ten vows, referred to as the Ten Non-Virtues or The Freedom Vows. They are referred to as "Freedom Vows" because the Buddha taught how to achieve a state of peace in life in the most expeditious way—in other words, how to make every day better. What works? What will you do? What will work for most everyone that, if practiced, will free them from illusion, attachment, and the resulting dissatisfaction?

The ten vows are grouped by the three gateways (body, speech, and mind). Of the ten, three are related to the body, three are related to the mind, and four are related to speech. They are:

Of the body

- Refrain from taking life or killing

- Refrain from taking things that don't belong to you or weren't freely given to you, or stealing

- Refrain from sexual misconduct

Of the speech

- Refrain from lying

- Refrain from divisive speech

- Refrain from harsh words

- Refrain from idle talk

Of the mind

- Refrain from covetousness

- Refrain from harmful thought or ill will

- Refrain from wrongs views

To Buddhists, the law of karma is inclusive of the motivation, or intention behind an act, not just the act itself. Therefore, when reflecting on different types of vows in Buddhist teachings, you will find that intention or motivation is an extremely important consideration. In some Bodhisattva teachings, it is sometimes necessary to commit to actions that appear to be contradictory to spiritual principles. In the section on the Five Precepts, we discussed how it is sometimes necessary to kill one person to save many others. The karma of such an action derives from the intention or motivation behind it.

One of the first and most contentious issues that come up when talking about the Freedom Vows and that is the first Freedom Vow of not to kill. This invariably raises questions about meat-eating, vegetarianism, and veganism. Before we get deeper into the Freedom Vows, let's look at this consistently controversial topic of meat-eating versus vegetarianism or veganism.

It has been reported that Adolf Hitler was a vegetarian and yet His Holiness The Dalai Lama eats meat for his health. Hitler, as a representative of embodied evil, is seemingly acting in a compassionate way and the Dalai Lama as a symbol of compassion, is taking life. We cannot accurately judge another person's intention based on outward behavior. And, equally, we need to take careful consideration of our intention.

In many primarily Buddhist countries like Tibet and Japan, vegetarianism is not predominant. Your food choices are an important part of spiritual reflection since food is at the center of all our lives.

Every item of food requires us to make choices based on awareness of interdependence, compassion, and the importance of supporting our own health and the health and well-being of others. Yet, the most important thing to remember about all Buddhist vows is that each person makes choices and takes action based on the intersection of multiple circumstances playing out in his or her life that we cannot know.

Some people refuse to eat red meat. Some people will not drink milk. Some people will eat what is served to them but limit their own purchases of animal products. Remember that the Buddha stressed that we should not accept his teachings on "blind faith" but rather should explore them for ourselves and make up our own minds. Whether we choose to be vegetarian is a decision each of us must make for ourselves, according to our time and place, our health or physical conditions, and other circumstances. If we do decide to eat fish, fowl, or meat, we may decide to avoid purchasing from sources that use inhumane practices in raising or slaughtering their animals.

The case of meat-eating versus vegetarianism is one of the most prickly issues in Buddhism when it comes to Right Action. But it, like all our actions, should be guided by Right View and Right Intention. Grounding ourselves in right view and right intention enables confidence in our own internal wisdom. If we continue to build the conditions that create and sustain right view, right intention will follow. And with right intention, our actions will be measured, not reactive and not concerned with external authority or the behaviors or others.

A first step in building a supportive view, the right view, that builds the foundation for right action is to look at The Freedom Vows as what to do and not what "thou shall not do." I really like this way of looking at the Freedom Vows. Shouldn't a vow be something that you strive to do, rather than something you feel admonished not to do?

In writing this now, I'm thinking about the vow I made and shared with you in the Right Speech section. The vow was not to post anything on social media that wasn't positive and that I wouldn't say in front of someone. I should have phrased it as "post only positive thoughts." Much easier and more motivating, isn't it?

Looking at it this way, the Freedom Vows would go like this:

Of the body:

- **Nourish life.**

     Do things to protect life. Did you move a pencil off the stairway that someone might have slipped on? You're not going to get a chance to throw someone out of the way of a speeding taxi or invent a vaccine every day. Did you give aspirin to someone at work? Did you make tea for someone with a sniffle? This is protecting life.

- **Honor people's property.**

     Did you take the last of the toilet paper from the bathroom and make sure it was replaced for the next person? Did you pick up that tiny piece of Kleenex that just fell out of your purse and put it in your pocket or purse to throw away later, or did you leave it on the floor? Stuff that small matters. Heaven is built on small things. An empty bucket can be filled by drops of water. You don't have to be Mother Teresa to have an impact on others' happiness.

- **Are you sexually pure (not necessarily celibate, but pure?) and are you faithful in your relationships with others?**

    If you are engaging in sex, are you obsessed about it or thinking about it all day, or doing it in improper places at improper times, and with improper people? A healthy sexual, normal, relationship is fine. Adultery, of course, is not. Does it bother your peace of mind? That's the question. Are you maintaining the level of sexual purity that you've committed to? For a married person it would be, did you check out someone else's partner today? Just for a second, did you think that way? Don't let it obsess your life. Honor your own and other people's commitments and don't ever cross that line.

Of the speech:

- **Be truthful.**

    Try to be totally truthful all day long. Are you required to tell someone how bad their dress looks if they ask you for your opinion? Change the subject. Drop your pencil or coffee cup. If it would hurt the person in some way, or make them very angry, or if it's very destructive, it's best to slide out of it, if you can. The key, again, is your intention. Would it hurt the other person or would it help them?

- **Do you speak in ways that bring people together?**

    Do you, in your everyday conversations, try to bring people close together? Once in a while, you meet a person who's really good at this. I have a friend who will run up to you and say, "I've got someone you have to meet! You'll love this person!" He introduces you and you become best friends. Do you see what I mean? Because our normal human tendency is, "Did you hear what he said about you?" Our tendency is to do the opposite. Find ways to bring people together with your words.

- **Speak gently. Gentle, thoughtful.**

  Don't talk trash talk at work to "be one of the guys" and expect to have a habit of gentle speech during the other hours. And don't talk in sweet ways when you're not feeling sweet at all. Like when you say, "Have a nice day," but what you really mean is "Go to hell." Your speech is judged by your intent. Speak gently and think gently.

- **Speak meaningfully.**

  Whenever you open your mouth, try to say something that has some kind of relevance to the person's life. Don't yap about the horrible thing a political or entertainment personality did. Or about stuff that doesn't matter, stuff that doesn't help anybody. Don't complain about people or things in the news or just waste talk, okay? Before you open your mouth, ask yourself if you're about to say something meaningful.

Of the mind:

- **When you see someone else achieve something or get something, be happy for them.**

  What's the opposite of that? It's like jealousy or unhappiness when somebody gets something nice. When something good happens to somebody else, you rush up and say, "I'm so happy you got that promotion! You really deserve it." Try to consciously experience the joy in other people's successes. Our human tendency is to be jealous. As budding bodhisattvas, we are committed to the goal of bringing every happiness to every sentient being. So, don't think, "I don't see why he got the promotion!"

- **Try to really feel for people suffering misfortune, no matter how famous they are or how much you don't like them.**

  When someone is suffering in some way, take the time and the effort to try to empathize with them. The normal human tendency is to do the opposite. "Oh, so-and-so got caught in bank fraud or a sexual scandal! His life is ruined! Tell me more!" There's this human tendency to be fascinated by other people's problems, especially famous people's problems.

  "So and so committed suicide? Why? How?" This is the big thing in social media and on cable TV. People seem to love to hear about the misfortune of others. You need to think the opposite way. When you hear about something like that, your thought should be, "Oh, I'm sorry for his family, and I feel really bad about it and I wish that wouldn't happen to anyone." It's the opposite of being fascinated by other people's problems. You truly try to put yourself in their place. Try to have extensive empathy or compassion for other people's problems, rather than this secret little joy about them. It's a weird human tendency. You're not upset by it, you are fascinated by it.

- **Maintain a Buddhist worldview.**

  Understand that all good things come from helping other people and bad things come from looking out for your own interests, only. You can watch out for your own interests, but equally, watch out for other people's interests.

Right Action Practice: Vow Tracking & The Pause

I recommend keeping a journal to track your thoughts, speech, and actions. This was a practice given by one of my teachers, originating from a practice done by Tibetan monks. The monks would go through the day and for each negative deed they committed, they would put a black stone in one pocket, and for each positive action, they would put a white stone in the other pocket. At the end of the day, they reviewed their stone totals and reflected on how they could do better.

You can do the same thing with a notebook or smartphone, checking yourself every two, three, or four hours. Pick one of the Freedom Vows to track all day. You note what you were thinking, saying, or doing in the last two- or four-hour period, before you've forgotten. You will be surprised at what you discover about yourself.

Not only does this practice build mindfulness into your day, but it is also very effective in correcting mindless habits that you wish you didn't have. If you commit to this practice for a long enough time you will notice a trend. You might notice that you repeat similar negative thoughts, speech, or actions throughout the day and from day-to-day. Don't be discouraged. Now that you are aware of it, you will form an intention to correct those actions.

This is where the pause comes in. You now know that you tend to repeat this behavior and you have the intention to stop it. That is all your mind needs to be watchful. Being alert helps you to observe what thoughts or feelings come before the behavior you're trying to curb. Then, the next time you notice the warning sign, you can pause.

Reflections on Right Action

Practice of the Path

Walking this path for years
I don't see it snaking
subtle left, wrap right
into wild.

I don't look for the perfect way,
never thought where
just walk—
practice of the path.

No self directing,
my stride continues on its own
until the scrub of white ash—
a gentle shoot bows to the sky.

Turning from the bounds
of walking, walker, destination,
being the path—
The path arrives at me.

~ Wendy Shinyo Haylett

-5-

RIGHT LIVELIHOOD: RIGHT LIVING

"Some people think that they will practice the dharma
once they have finished with their worldly business.
This is a mistaken attitude because our work in the world NEVER
finishes. Work is like a ripple of water continually moving on the
surface of the ocean. It is very difficult
to break free from our occupations in order to practice
the Dharma. The busy work with which we fill
our lives is only completed at the time of our death."

— *Geshe Kelsang Gyatso, from "Meaningful to Behold"*

I BELIEVE WHEN THE BUDDHA SPOKE OF RIGHT LIVELIHOOD HE WAS SPEAKING MORE ABOUT RIGHT LIVING, not necessarily about "livelihood" or work, as we would think of livelihood.

I am frequently disappointed in both the amount written about Right Livelihood and the quality of what is written or taught. Until recently, much of it doesn't seem relatable. It doesn't really speak to what I think many of us struggle with, in our day-to-day working lives.

The Buddha seemed to teach less about right livelihood than of the other steps on the path. He taught basic concepts but consistently stressed how everything hinges on Right View. I will paraphrase his teachings from *The Middle Length Discourses of the Buddha* (*Majjhima Nikaya*).

He taught that we should avoid livelihoods based on scheming, belittling (are you listening politicians and TV commentators?), usury (loan shark), and he singled out professions that bring harm, including dealing in weapons, intoxicants and poison, killing, cheating, prostitution, and slavery.

The emphasis on Right View is clear in the Buddha's teachings to avoid livelihoods affected by taints (something that defiles, contaminates, or pollutes us). If our view of things is tainted, we could begin to see things in a way that seems right, even if it is wrong or is something that would lead to suffering and, therefore, goes against his prescribed path to the absence of suffering.

The Buddha directed laypeople to be skillful and energetic, to protect their income from thieves, to have good friends and be generous to them, and to live within their means. I think this supports my claim that the Buddha was really teaching about "right living." And, in his teaching in The Middle Length Discourses, he consistently turned the focus on right thought, right effort, and right mindfulness as those that "run and circle around right livelihood."

He also made clear that right livelihood is that part of our lives where the Eightfold Path comes together as a focus of practice if we want to be happy in our work. In other words, we need to know the wisdom teachings to understand who we are at work; the morality teachings to know how to relate to the work we do, who we work with and for; and the mental discipline teachings to work in a way that brings us the most happiness.

As a career coach, I work with people every day whose work lives cause them significant unhappiness, stress, or general dissatisfaction. Just mentioning right livelihood probably makes a lot of you squirm. Either you question the "rightness" of your livelihood or thinking about your livelihood makes you feel stress. If you're like most of us—including me, many times throughout my life—it seems that life is work, pay the bills, sleep, then work. Lather, rinse, repeat.

This is the unsatisfactoriness or "suffering" of life. But, as David Brazier says in *The Feeling Buddha*, "The path to enlightenment begins with facing the reality of affliction." And, let's face it, many of us feel that our livelihoods are our afflictions. Yet, most of us spend most of our waking hours either preparing to go to work, going there, being there, and getting over being there when we get home. What does this say about the happiness level in our culture? The Buddha said that what we all have in common is our desire to be happy.

So, are we doing time working for our economic security? Or are we working at becoming the person that has their own internal security of happiness? We are working to have—or to become—but we're generally not being with our work, authentically, mindfully.

Right now, you're all imagining the robed monastics sitting in meditation or doing walking meditation. You may be thinking that that's right livelihood. We may have this thought of mindful non-doing but statues of *Kuan Yin*, the lay bodhisattva of compassion, belie that belief. *Kuan Yin* statues hold working tools, like trowels, in each of her thousand hands. And this is a testament to how the Buddha valued work and a commitment to our economic responsibilities.

Right livelihood isn't just about how we earn money, but about finding the right lifestyle that will further great work, right work, by you or others.

Work! Is It Just About Work?

Studies have shown—and my own role as a career coach supports this—that millions of Americans experience at least some degree of job dissatisfaction. Corporations continue to downsize, meaning "upsizing" the stress on employees with more work and more frequent deadline pressure, combined with job insecurity.

I don't know about your circumstances, but I imagine many of you feel your jobs aren't fulfilling—or worse—stressful and exhausting. Either you aren't able to engage your creativity, skills, and abilities or your boss or co-workers are demanding, unfriendly, or aggressive.

Or, if you're an entrepreneur, even if you are the boss and can set your own hours, you may be stressed by not enough or too many clients, not enough income, or discovering you are not doing what you really thought you would be doing and like to do, but instead, you are being an administrator. If you are conscientious, you are likely to be scrutinizing your fees and services on a regular basis, balancing fairness to your clients with fairness to yourself and your own economic security.

The service economy has become a predominant driver in the overall American economy, and it has attracted many entrepreneurs and soloprenuers due to the relative ease of starting an Internet service or product business. And what that means is competition. And competition brings with it all sorts of decisions about right livelihood including marketing to attract a client base, but marketing that provides value without "giving away the store."

As an employee, manager, business owner, or solopreneur, we all face difficult questions:

- How can we earn enough money to engage in work we enjoy without sacrificing our peace of mind, or health, or our spiritual values?

- How can we contribute our unique talents without harming other beings or the environment?

- How can we avoid the endless cycle of speed and greed that is our cultural tone?

The decision of profession today carries a burden of continuous questions and nagging doubts. In some ways, life was much simpler in the time of the Buddha, 2,600 years ago. Harder material circumstances, but simpler maybe because they didn't have to deal with amazing and often overwhelming choices we now have in life. I think we need to cut ourselves some slack and resign ourselves to the fact that no matter what profession we choose, it will come with a messy mix of good and bad consequences.

Yet, our jobs offer us the opportunity to practice by maximizing the good and minimizing the bad. We can't run away from our connection to the rest of the world, especially in a global economy. But we can ask ourselves if we are "doing time" working for our economic security or are we working at becoming the person that will provide that security to more than just ourselves.

This question extends beyond what we contribute through our work and to the way we contribute to all those our work touches, on and off the job. We need to move from thinking about work as what we have, or what we are becoming on our progression up the ladder, to how and who we are being with our work. Are we authentic? Are we mindful?

If you think about it, why did the Buddha address livelihood in the first place? A monk is not concerned with that. A monk's livelihood is about begging, meditating, and keeping ethical behavior. So, Right Livelihood is primarily a lay concern. And, in our Western culture, most Buddhist practitioners are like you and me. We are not monks; we are householders trying to incorporate the teachings of right livelihood in our day-to-day world.

In thinking about right livelihood, I think most of us immediately think about "what" livelihood? What career, industry, or function? A career devoted to social change, ethics, environmental stability? Or creative work that allows direct expression of passions and talents? Or maybe just a good job for a fair wage?

One of my podcast listeners asked if there is a way to think about how we choose to make a living? She added that she's made a career of working in the nonprofit world but is struggling with the person for whom she works.

That is a very good question and expands the focus. Right livelihood implies way more than just the occupation but also asks you to question your intention. Ask yourself what you bring to the job, it's employees, your managers, and its customers or clients? What are your thoughts when you're at the job and your thoughts about the job when you go home? If negative thoughts result from any of those relationships, it is good to examine it from the perspective of right livelihood, but also the perspective of right view and right thoughts or intention.

I would suggest that right livelihood isn't just about how we earn money, but about finding the right lifestyle and attitude that will further great work, or right work, by you or others. As I mentioned before, the Buddha emphasized right livelihood as the aspect where all parts of the Eightfold Path come together. This is where our practice can really be pumped!

First as a student, then as a teacher and lay minister with a focus on everyday spirituality, I was able to change my perspective and connect what lay ministry meant to me in my work. Instead of trying to imitate monastic practice, my unique value as a lay minister of everyday spirituality is in the practice I do in my life as a householder, as a someone who works for a living. My lay life is the perfect practice. Lay life is the perfect vehicle to live the Dharma.

For most of us, work is the golden opportunity to walk the walk, not just talk the talk. We spend most of our waking hours at work. This is where we are presented with all the tough choices about Right View, Right Intention, Right Speech, and Right Action. This is where we can most easily practice mindfulness, but where we may be the most likely not to!

Another podcast listener wrote with this question: "At present (and for some time now), I struggle in the work environment to practice skillful thought, speech, and action." And he added that he "would benefit from your continued sharing on how to apply Buddhist principles in the workplace. How to sit with fear of failure, inferiority, frustration with others. We need mindfulness in the workplace badly. Myself included."

I answered both listeners by reminding them about the emphasis the Buddha put on Right View and Right Intention. A lot of this has to do with what I shared about how I needed a change of perspective to see how my work could become my perfect Dharma practice. Remember, the practice is not just what activity or organization you're contributing to, but how you are contributing to the people you work with.

I work with clients on a weekly basis who struggle with their bosses and co-workers. Many times, when we look at the situation together, the emotions are diffused, the frustrations and anger are diffused—jumbled together in a cloud of discontent or unhappiness and we are unable to pinpoint who and what is causing the problems or suffering they feel. In those instances, I try to lead the client away from a purely subjective understanding of "me" versus "him" or "her" and to a "bigger" perspective that includes understanding why that obnoxious boss or co-worker is the way they are.

In looking more at the situation as a movie or book, with no subjective buy-in, my clients typically see things differently, which helps interrupt the stories they tell themselves about their work situation, and it enables them to try to create right livelihood out of the work they've been given.

This is helping to create a feeling of wanting what we already have versus wanting what we don't have. One of the ways we can do that is to transform our work life into our spiritual practice. If we can begin to view work without clinging to a personal or selfish sense of what we think we need, want, or deserve, then we can practice adapting an attitude of dynamic acceptance, which transcends the small view of "my boss is a jerk." Your boss, or your co-worker, may, indeed, be a jerk, but can you apply the right view of interconnectedness, right intention, right speech, and right action to your work? Can you transform your work into your spiritual practice?

It is in asking the hard questions and making the tough decisions that arise in family and work-life that we find our practice. The questions about whether we're using skillful means when interacting with bosses and co-workers and in balancing, or juggling, time and money. It is this very struggle that is our practice.

I frequently hear Buddhists express that they wish they could go on a three-year retreat, or become a monk, or some other daydream that makes them feel that they would then be true practitioners, true Buddhists. And I hear coaching clients wish they weren't working in the for-profit field, but in the non-profit, and those in non-profit wishing the bottom line didn't matter so much. But these are all indications that we aren't bringing Right View to Right Livelihood. Unless we have the right awareness of the suffering, stress, or dis-ease our work is meant to allay, we won't see the meaning in it.

There is a Sufi saying, "Praise Allah, and tie your camel to the post." This is right livelihood. We need to do what we need to do, but we need to do it mindfully, fully connected to our inner wisdom that will enable us to see every opportunity to benefit others and avoid opportunities that might harm.

We need to be clear about what we're thinking and what we're doing. Why are we doing what we're doing? We need to think like this when engaged in any activity: "Am I doing this for myself or for others?" Even if the others are our family or a pet. Because we know from the Dharma that everything and everyone is interconnected and that there are no self-existent causes or identities, we can remember that *everything* we do is related to others.

The clearest, most in-your-face teaching of this, for me, comes from Geshe Kelsang Gyatso in the quote from his commentary on Shantideva's *Way of the Bodhisattva*, *Meaningful to Behold* that I opened the chapter with. It's not about waiting until we finish this project, or get this much money, or retire, or some other far-flung goal because as Geshe Gyatso wrote, *"Our work in the world never finishes."*

So, let's talk about what we do. What do you do and how tied to your title or what you do are you? How much of your identity comes from it? Many people can't even answer these questions unless they lose their job and then they see it and it becomes obvious. Let's explore how our identity is connected to our jobs, looking at who we are versus what we do.

I Am ≠ I Do

How much of your identity is connected to what you do for a living? Through coaching unemployed and underemployed clients and from my personal experience having to leave a career due to illness, I intimately know how tight that connection is.

In the late 1980s and early 1990s, I went through a crisis of identity—a crisis of "not doing." I had been forced by a chronic autoimmune disease, Systemic Lupus, to leave a successful career in television broadcasting. I was 39 and had been a television engineer since I was 19. I was a television engineer almost as soon as I was an adult and I didn't know who I was if I wasn't a television engineer.

Like many people, my identity was connected to what I did, rather than who I was. And something bigger, more powerful— something my ego couldn't control—took that identity away from me. Combined with the double-blow of a loss of occupational identity and loss of income, was the missing productivity. Nothing to "do."

In our society, doing is being. Our days and nights are scheduled like 24x7, high-volume manufacturing operations, with our value reflected to us by our capacity for doing and our ability for continuous delivery. Faced with non-scheduled days and zero output, my whole being seemed in question. And the more I fought the stillness, the sicker I became. It is at that point, my authentic Self, my true Being, my Buddha Nature, began to whisper—then shout—to get my attention. This whispering came as teachings from myself to myself.

The lessons began in January 1992 as interruptions of daily journal entries. A life-long journal writer, I would confide my physical pain, guilt, anger, sadness, regret, desires, and wishes to those blank pages. The writing was self-absorbed and ego-focused until January of 1992 when another voice or thought, like a mistuned radio, began to interfere with what I thought I was going to write.

"There is nothing to find that you weren't given when you were born" was the second lesson. Everything I ever needed was given to me when I was born. The reassurance of that lesson, and all the lessons that came after, slowed me down long enough to look inside. And I recognized, or rediscovered, my true self or my Buddha Nature.

I found or discovered this peace by being forced to slow down. Slowing down reconnected me to the happy, curious, trusting child I had always been—hidden behind the person or different people I had tried to become. In looking through the eyes of that child, I remembered magical occurrences.

I remembered being five years old, lying in bed and waiting for my special friend, a little wizard, to fly out from between the ballerinas in my pink and gold wallpaper. Many nights he would come to visit, bringing shelves of big, beautiful leather-bound books in gold leaf, filled with the secrets of the universe and hovering mid-air above me. I remembered thinking that I must be too young to understand the books because when I reached up to take one, the books, the shelves, and the wizard disappeared. But the wizard's promise was kept.

My wizard (who I now refer to as *Manjushri*, the Bodhisattva representing "wisdom" or "insight") reappeared 34 years later in those journal teachings when I slowed down enough to hear. He revealed a secret to me: I AM DOES NOT EQUAL I DO!

The problem with equating our "selfs" with what we do is that it positions our very being as an object and creates a me-me conflict if we are not passionately aligned with—or love—our work. It is self versus the other of who we are as our occupation or our concept of what that occupation represents from an external societal value. Doing something doesn't make me be that something. Common sense assures me of that. But I act as though—I feel as though—that is the case.

I do this. You do that. "I'm not the boss; you are." "I'm this; you're not." It starts very young. Adults innocently ask young children what they want to be when they grow up, focusing them beyond the now, beyond their being and on to becoming something else. It creates a culture of competition, not cooperation. I can't help but think it programs young minds into believing they must be something other than what they are. And creates a subtle feeling that who they are is not quite enough.

The other complication to I am=I do is that what we do today is completely removed from any direct connection to the resultant "goodness" it brings to others or the world. I think the biggest challenge to us today is we are so removed from any good that comes from what we do. It's more about the doing and less about the why and what we're doing.

We are not a simple society or a small village, but a global economy. We rarely see that we are contributing anything useful with our work. We feel like we are working for money, or the mortgage payment, or the health insurance bill. Therefore, we see what we do as utilitarian and not as a contribution to the greater good.

This is expected really. It's hard to determine the absolute value of anything. The price of gold and the value of a dollar, stocks, and bonds rise and fall. The prices of products on the marketplace rise and fall. The monetary value of anything, including you and your job, is based on a supply-and-demand economy. And that is what establishes value. Even our own value.

Value is determined by the cars we drive, the clothes we wear, the houses we live in, and the stuff we have. Sometimes we take jobs and buy things to maintain an image of value. That is why many of us feel dead or alienated in the right livelihood part of the Eightfold path.

But if we remember Right View, applying the wisdom teachings of impermanence and a lack of a permanent self then the certainty of who we are becomes shaky. We are who we are in the moment. What you do is what you're doing at this moment, then what you're doing in the next moment.

It's best to keep a broader out-of-the-self-you-think-you-are perspective in appreciating what you do. You do many things during the course of your workday and at home. And if you focus on doing each of those things with Right Intention, your livelihood—your life—will have the value of each thing you contribute to your co-workers, your company, your customers and clients, your family, your friends, and your neighbors.

Practicing Right Livelihood as Lifestyle

Earlier in my Buddhist practice, all I could think about was how I couldn't do Vajrayana practice and how I couldn't do days and weeks of meditation. I became focused on personal failure. I was grasping at what I wasn't! Then I had an awakening of sorts. I was able to see the connection between my personal life and my work life as an evolution to a "perfect design" of my life as my practice.

I was able to see how if it wasn't for illness, I wouldn't have had the time to get to know myself, to be comfortable with that self and rest in my perfect-as-it-is Buddha Nature. And if it wasn't for me being able to discover the ever-present stability of who I was at my center, I wouldn't have attempted writing, coaching, or practicing Buddhism. I began viewing my life and my work as a coach and writer AS my monk's duties.

We are clearly not living in a time where our choices are simple, yet that shouldn't be an excuse not to try! We need to take small steps, look for tiny opportunities to practice right livelihood in our time at work and in our time off. Even the smallest right choice can make a big difference.

We can make choices about what jobs we take, of course, but also in an interconnected, right-living way, we can think about the other jobs or livelihoods we support through our purchases of cars, clothes, food, and investments. We can think about the consequences of buying the cheapest item if it was produced in a sweatshop. We can question whether our purchases and investments are contributing to the destruction of rainforests or the extinction of species. We can question whether we should buy the products made in other countries that continually violate human rights.

Does this mean all at once? Absolutely not! Our culture and economy are bound together in a complex, interconnected puzzle. It takes a dogged persistence to investigate, evaluate, then make good choices. It also takes time to overcome our own habits and desires.

We can contribute to changes in the world related to right livelihood. We've seen shareholder withdrawal of South African investments lead to the collapse of Apartheid. And how environmental groups are gradually accomplishing elimination of the use of Styrofoam at fast-food chains.

We all have opportunities to make a difference every day. Even a small activity to reduce suffering or increase compassion can help. The way you answer the phone will embody right livelihood, the way you talk to a client or a co-worker, the way you file, the way you walk to and from a meeting. Do we try—honestly try—to take care of our co-workers and customers? Or are we just doing our job?

Do we live in ways that help others be peaceful and happy? Do we live in ways that help ourselves be peaceful and happy? This sounds simple, but this is right livelihood. To start, ask yourself how you spend your free time. Our time is part of our wealth and part of Buddhist practice is generosity or sharing our wealth—our dollars and our time. Ask yourself: "do I spend my free time entertaining myself, primarily—escaping—or am I spending some time contributing to my own and others' enrichment and fulfillment?

Are you taking care of yourself, through meditation, exercise, or creative endeavors that contribute to your own and others' enjoyment? Are you spending time with your family and friends? Are you taking a course? Are you spending time helping at a church, Dharma Center, community center, or volunteer organization?

We will each have a different formula that works for us. But whatever your individual distribution of time, your life needs to be more than work. And, if like most of us, you need to work most of the time, try to be as mindful as possible while you are working.

Be aware of how you're thinking while you're working. Are you focused on what you're getting or not getting rather than what you're giving? Do you have an attitude of caring that includes self-care and care for your co-workers, employers, and customers? Do you look for ways to give more or be more cooperative?

We need to have this view and be teachers of this view to help transform our society from transactional to cooperative. It takes a shift in the mass consciousness that starts with a shift in each of our thinking. A shift can be realized in each of us—and all of us— by our commitment to a cooperative rather than competitive view in all aspects of our lives. This cooperative view is the intention needed to make everything we do meaningful.

This can be done by working together. This can be done by overcoming our virtual culture where everything is about me and my phone or me and my computer. Sharing, community, hospitality, and generosity are the ingredients of a non-alienated society that works together for things that matter.

You can create this kind of community or society by being a part of one. And when you do, you are practicing the Buddha's teaching of the emptiness of self and the interconnection of all beings. What makes our work, our livelihood, and our lives "right" is not only about the nature of the work or activities, but of the qualities of our hearts and minds that we bring to our work.

Right Livelihood Practice: Five Daily Guidelines

As I wrote about in the previous reflection, right livelihood is deeper and broader than just work. It is right living. Living with an understanding of how everything you do touches every being in the world. The practice of Five Daily Life Guidelines offered by The Bright Dawn Center of Oneness Buddhism will help transform simple daily habits into right living. By using this practice to observe and guide your thoughts and behavior—in your work and when you're not working—you will be practicing right living. I offer deep bows of gratitude to Rev. Koyo Kubose for this practice and for letting me share it in this book.

Five Daily Life Guidelines:

- **CONSUME MINDFULLY:** Eat sensibly and don't be wasteful. Pause before buying; see if breathing is enough. Pay attention to the effects of media consumed.

- **SHARE LOVING-KINDNESS:** Consider other people's views deeply. Work for peace at every level. Spread joy, not negativity.

- **PRACTICE GRATITUDE:** Respect the people encountered; they are our teachers. Be equally grateful for opportunities and challenges. Notice where help is needed and be quick to act.

- **DISCOVER WISDOM:** Find connections between teachings and daily life. Do not become attached to conclusions. Mute the judgmental tongue.

- **ACCEPT CONSTANT CHANGE:** Be open to whatever arises in every moment. Cultivate "Beginner's Mind." Keep going, keep going.

Note: You can find the above on the central website of Bright Dawn: http://www.brightdawn.org/. Then click on the tab, "Spiritual Resources" where you will find a drop-down menu, "Daily Dharma."

Reflection on Right Livelihood

Spirit of Place

Our neighbors on this earth: woods, rivers, and fields always welcome us to their magnificent homes. Coming from neighborhoods where streams are paved, our anxious steps are slowed, disciplined by stalks, rocks, and stems, forcing our attention to earth, sky, and branches bowing to meet us. The ground, littered with shed feathers, the stirring of long-legged spiders, and wooly bears on the move; the sky, a goldfinch drills a stem for seed, chickadees swoop, and chattering sparrows dart from tree to tree—we don't understand what they're saying, but we know it's the source of our strength. The spirits of the land aren't lost, they're just waiting for people to hang around long enough to know them. Seeing, hearing and knowing what others can't or won't say—a bed of moss, crickets scampering, grasses whitened by harsh frost, bees gliding—a transformative power hidden in your attention to their gracious and magical universe, where the stains of an artificial environment are washed by a spirit of place that recognizes itself.

~ Wendy Shinyo Haylett

PART THREE: APPRECIATION • MEDITATION

-6-

RIGHT EFFORT: FIND A JOYFUL BALANCE

"It's important when we're practicing to have this mind of delight and to really try and deliberately cultivate it. We Westerners sometimes have a hard time with that because we tend to get effort confused with pushing. We go from the extreme of pushing to the other extreme of just being lackadaisical, lazy, and apathetic. We don't seem to get this middle way of taking delight.

Both the laziness and the pushing, neither of them has much delight in them. When we're lazy, we're not taking delight in the Dharma; we're just going "Ughhh!" When we're pushing, we're into our Protestant work ethic culture—we've got to achieve, attain and "Let's go for it!" That doesn't bring about this relaxed mental state that we need for practice. It's working with our mind and having this positive aspiration so that the practice really becomes a delight."

— Thubten Chodron, from series of teachings based on the "The Gradual Path to Enlightenment" (Lamrim)
https://thubtenchodron.org/1994/07/generate-effort-wisdom/

THE WORD "EFFORT" CAN CONNOTE A SERIOUS OR EVEN SOUR PRACTICE. Depending on the person, you can either be turned on or turned off by beginning an activity or starting a practice that will require effort. Yes, effort is associated with positive results like dieting to lose weight; exercising to tone your body, get in shape, and feel better; eating right for health or the health of our planet; and meditating for psychological and spiritual balance.

The word "effort" like the word "labor" carries a Protestant-Work-Ethic sting for me. But if you study the available teachings on Right Effort, the first thing you will notice is that it's referred to by quite a few different words. You will see it referred to as "diligence" or "enthusiasm" and, also, "joyous effort." I decided on joyful balance because I think it expresses the right intent for our Everyday Buddhism approach.

As you can see, by the varying labels applied to this part of the path, the sense of effort as in labor is not really the point. From our everyday perspective, it rests heavily on the first and most important step of the Eightfold Path, Right View.

Certain parts of the Eightfold Path are based on wisdom, certain parts made of ethics, and the other parts, on meditation. But it is Right View that is the main support. As a review, the eight spokes of the wheel representing the eightfold path are Right View, Right Intention, Right Speech, Right Action, Right Livelihood, Right Effort, Right Mindfulness, and Right Concentration.

The first two (Right View and Right Intention) are grouped under the wisdom category. The next three, under ethics, which is Right Speech, Right Action, and Right Livelihood. And the last three, under meditation: Right Effort, Right Mindfulness, and Right Concentration.

AWARENESS: Right View & Right Intention

In the scheme I'm using for this book, I group the first two (Right View and right intention) under the concept of "awareness." Having "right" or the most helpful sense of awareness is wisdom. Wisdom is formed from Right View. Right

View is the awareness of the fact that all things in life are impermanent, recognition of the fact that life is constant change, and the understanding that we are not (and no one else is) the fixed self we think we or they are, but we are all the result of causes and conditions changing each moment and changing us.

It's also about being aware that grasping at the things we desire or pushing away the things that we have aversion to is not going to help us or anyone else be happier. Knowing this helps us form right intention, meaning setting our course every day based on the awareness that life is as it is. Life is suchness.

ACCEPTANCE: Right Speech, Right Action & Right Livelihood

The next three, normally grouped under ethics, I have referred to as "acceptance." They are right speech, right action, and right livelihood. To live a life with less dissatisfaction or more happiness, a certain amount of acceptance is necessary. This is not a passive, I-give-up type of acceptance. But a positive and strong—noble—acceptance of life the way it is. With that mindset and commitment, our speech, action, and livelihood (or living) are guided on a "right" or efficient and effective course to create more happiness for ourselves and others. When we face life with noble acceptance, we are less likely to get caught up behaviors driven by the three poisons of desire or grasping, aversion, and delusion.

APPRECIATION: Right Effort, Right Mindfulness & Right Concentration

The last three spokes of the Eightfold Path are categorized under the term "meditation", I refer to as "appreciation." They are right effort, right mindfulness, and right concentration. When we have awareness and acceptance of life as it is, appreciation naturally flows. Life is pretty OK most of the time if we're not wishing it was something different: Grasping at people and things we want, pushing people and things we don't want away from us, or being confused and deluded by thoughts of life being other than it is, then having to consistently wake up to the truth of things as they are.

We will begin looking at the Appreciation or Meditation category, with Right Effort.

The Four Aspects of Right Effort: Try To Do

Energy (*viriya*) is the mental factor behind right effort and it can be expressed in either positive or negative, wholesome or unwholesome forms. The same energy can power desire, aggression, violence, and ambition -OR- generosity, self-discipline, kindness, concentration, and understanding. For energy to be a positive contributor to your practice, or desire to rid yourself of discontentment, it needs the guidance of Right View and Right Intention.

The most basic, traditional definition of Right Effort is to exert oneself to develop wholesome qualities and remove unwholesome qualities.

The Buddha taught that there are **four aspects to Right Effort:**

- The effort to **prevent unwholesome qualities**, especially greed, anger, and ignorance, from arising.

- The effort to **extinguish unwholesome qualities** that have already arisen.

- The effort to **cultivate skillful, or wholesome, qualities**, especially generosity, loving-kindness, and wisdom (the opposites of greed, anger, and ignorance) that have not yet arisen.

- The effort to **strengthen the wholesome qualities** that have already arisen.

So, what is this type of effort about? Let's boil it down to the secret sauce of our Everyday Buddhism approach. The effort we're talking about is noticing the bad things you tend to think about or do, then trying to do something about them. Then, noticing the good qualities you would like to adopt and then trying to practice them or strengthen them.

Let's rephrase the Four Aspects this way:

- Notice areas in your life where you realize you are tempted to or that you participate in greedy, angry, or ignorant thinking or behavior, or in grasping, fear, or hatred. Even if just for a minute or even if you are going along with the crowd (or another person).

- Notice the things that you think, speak, or do on a more frequent basis. These habits are your own afflictions or *kleshas*. (Remember a *klesha* is a mental state that clouds the mind and manifests in unwholesome actions like anxiety, fear, anger, jealousy, desire, depression, etc.). Notice when you tend to do them, thinking about what triggers you to do them, then try to short-circuit or lessen the intensity of the triggers, so that you don't do them or don't do them as much. Right effort is not about trying to be perfect but about trying to be just a little better acting in alignment with your intentions. Trying not to do them as much helps us to succeed because instead of thinking we won't do them, then getting frustrated when we fail, we know we are trying, so we keep trying.

- Notice areas in your life where you could try to build better habits or a stronger practice in being more generous, loving, and wise, which are the opposites of greed, anger, and ignorance.

- Notice where and when you do pretty good in any of the good qualities like generosity, loving-kindness, and wisdom, and try to do them more often or do more of them.

The point of practicing Right Effort is about trying to be a better person. Remember, the Eightfold Path is an integrated holistic system, not a linear path. Central to right effort is the whole of the Eightfold Path with right view and right intention like the wind and the rudder helping the forward movement of effort to try to be a better person or at least less of a jerk.

The Five Hindrances: Try Not To Do

"Wrong effort" is defined as directing our energy into harmful, destructive trains of thought that distract us and make it difficult, if not impossible, to be mindful of or remember our intention. **The sutra teachings present the things that impede our concentration as the Five Hindrances:**

- Sensual desire

- Ill will

- Dullness and drowsiness

- Restlessness and worry

- Doubt

Sensual Desire

Sensual Desire and Ill Will are paired because they are both desires. Sensual desire wants something and ill will does not want something. Sensual desire and ill will are the strongest and represent greed and aversion at their core. The other three hindrances are less toxic, but still obstacles to remembering our intention. They represent the delusion at their core.

Sensual desire is frequently interpreted in two ways. In the narrow sense, it is described as lust for the "five strands of sense pleasure." This refers to agreeable sights, sounds, smells, tastes, and touches. More broadly, it is sometimes taught that it's not just lust for the "five strands" but any intensity of craving for sense pleasures, wealth, power, position, fame, or anything else craving grips on to.

I would add comfort and needing things to always go our way to the list of things classified as sensual desire. Comfort is an insidious craving that I would describe as a first-world craving. Many of our lives are very comfortable. So comfortable that a few weeks, days, or hours of discomfort and we're miserable and more focused on ourselves than normal. Of course, I know many don't have the problem of too much comfort, if you're striving to keep the electricity on or don't have electricity at all, but many of us in the West are addicted to comfort. I know I am and readily admit to a flare-up of crankiness if faced with too many days of heat and humidity, cold and snow, darkness and rain, and on and on. Heck, I can get immediately irritated if the Internet goes down for a few minutes.

Now before you think I'm telling you to ignore or isolate yourself from somatic experiences, I'm not. It's not about not noticing or appreciating bodily experiences as a wonderful part of your life, but about avoiding grasping at them so much so that they become what you focus on.

This obstacle is like trying to concentrate on something, our work for example, but our concentration gets distracted by thoughts, such as, "I want to check Twitter" or "I should look at that Facebook group", or "I really *need* a pickle or a piece of chocolate." (And if you're like me, I sometimes have cravings for both of those at the same time. And, no, I'm not pregnant).

Sensory pleasures or desires don't have to be big ones like lust but can be as normal and every-day as wanting to eat even when you're not hungry or wanting to be distracted by social media because you're bored, and so on. We need to put effort into identifying what we are inclined to crave or fall into the habit of doing, even if we don't want to do them, so that we are better able to stop the urge or desire as soon as it comes up.

Ill Will

The second hindrance, ill will, is a synonym for aversion. Aversion can be hatred, anger, resentment, or repulsion, whether directed towards other people, oneself, objects, or situations. The key to understanding this type of aversion in the way intended is that it is an aversion motivated by hostility or a wanting to either strike out and attack or pull away.

We can have an aversion toward a food that makes us ill or an aversion to being around a person who is foul-mouthed or abusive. Either of these are protective and not ill will. But if we have an aversion toward a person or people that is motivated by hostility, we can become so focused on it that it shuts us down or restricts our life, narrowing our minds and closing our hearts. And some people seem to thrive on the feeling. They become so focused on their hatred or resentment toward someone or a group of people that it becomes part of their purpose in life.

You don't have to look very far to see how political figures or political stances can cause aversion in people on the other side. And our media—social, broadcast and print—fans the flames of this ill will to expand its audience base and fill its coffers. This kind of aversion distorts and distracts life as it really is and people as they really are.

Some people depend on desire and aversion as their purpose or meaning. Desire and aversion energize and motivate them. Without it, life would seem flat. They are so focused on their objects of desire and ill will that they don't see life all around them. And, if they find kindred spirits who share in the same type of desire and aversion, they bond in a community that perpetuates both.

Before you think you can let this one go and not look too hard at it, ill will is part of all our lives. It doesn't have to be as compelling or crippling as I just described. It can be much more subtle. If you have a feeling of ill will towards someone, a group of people, or an organization, there can be a tendency to grasp at it, despite the discomfort it causes. It's a subtle wishing for the other to suffer as you have perceived they have caused you suffering.

This is a natural reaction and not a reason to beat yourself up over it, but it is a reason to be mindful of it—watch it arising and passing away, curiously investigating what triggers the feeling and where that feeling comes from.

Another way to help ill will lose its hold is to be aware of it arising in you then quickly switch to thinking about or doing something that is truly meaningful and helpful to someone. It might be too much to ask you to extend a wish toward the object of your ill that they will have happiness and be free from suffering right at first, but the more you can bypass grasping at ill will by doing something meaningful, the more likely you are to arrive at the place where you can wish the object of your hostility peace and happiness.

Dullness and Drowsiness

The third hindrance, dullness and drowsiness, is a compound of two factors linked together by their common feature of mental ineffectiveness. One is dullness, which is described as having mental inertia, the other is drowsiness, mental sinking, heaviness of mind, or an excessive inclination to sleep.

The fourth hindrance is the opposite: restlessness and worry. Restlessness is agitation or excitement, which drives the mind from thought to thought with speed and frenzy. Worry is remorse over past mistakes, anxiety about their possible undesired consequences, and an inordinate focus on the future.

The third and fourth seem like epidemics in our culture. In our always-on, 24x7, everything-is-breaking-news that is delivered instantly to our phones, our minds are either put to sleep or agitated. If you've ever tried to meditate you are intimately familiar with both the states: mind heaviness and mind frenzy. But check it for yourself, in your everyday life—not when you're meditating—and see if you're also going through those states as you're doing whatever you're doing. You can be bored while working and agitated while relaxing.

Something I try to remember when I catch myself thinking I'm bored or feeling frenzied is to do something other than what I'm doing, which is usually to pick up my phone or switch to the browser tab with Twitter open on it, is this: What did I do back before the Internet and smartphones? Yes, I was an adult then and I remember sitting and working without the constant urge to do something else. It is possible. I remember long hours at my desk working, studying, or writing, with the only distraction being watching a bird out my window.

Another method I use is to think about people before TV and the news was delivered hourly or daily. They just did their days. That's it. They did what was in front of them. It's only a habit. It is not a need to know, but a habit. Do you really need to know what is going on everywhere in the world right this minute or even today? How will that help you, your family, or your friends?

On to the fifth hindrance, or doubt. When doubt is taught as the fifth hindrance, it is not the doubt required by a critical intelligence or wisdom, which the Buddha encourages, but the kind of doubt that manifests as a chronic indecisiveness and lack of resolution. It is a persistent inability to commit oneself. I believe this hindrance, too, has been strengthened by our culture of constant exposure to successful business figures, actors, celebrities, artists, writers, etc. We doubt ourselves because our world—our culture through all media—is holding up all these people as the shining examples of "perfect." Which means we're not perfect, right? We're not even close, so why try?

These people we see in media are caricatures of themselves. We see only their richness, their success, their beauty. We don't see who they really are. We don't know about their worries or doubts.

The opposite is also true. We see all the ugliness and meanness in our world, and we think "What's the use? Why should I even try to be a better person? Why should I even try to help?"

I won't go too far down the rabbit hole of each of these expressions of self-doubt and the path of our cultural mean-spiritedness, but it seems that the constant media bombardment of the caricature-like good and the caricature-like bad of the world, and all the people in it, could be contributing factors to despair and self-loathing.

The ideal of perfection presented by social media tends to exasperate any thoughts we have of our failures or unworthiness. And the constant drumbeat of misery, violence, war, and disaster can create despair in even the most positive of us.

This doubt clouds our ability to look at the world and ourselves without judgment, causing us to expect to see things the way we have been brainwashed to believe they are rather than the way things really are. A technique I use when doubt begins to overwhelm me is to step out my back door and watch anything in nature: an ant, a bird, a squirrel, or a leaf on a branch. Observe the complete naturalness of an ant on its journey or a squirrel hopping from tree to tree. The natural trust in things being as they are keeps that ant on its path and the squirrel free from fear despite the length and height of the jump. We are made of the same stuff and that natural trust exists at the core of us, in our Buddha Nature.

The Three Types of Destructive Thinking

Beyond the Five Hindrances, traditional teachings outline three major destructive ways of thinking:

- Thinking covetously

- Thinking with malice

- Thinking with antagonism

Thinking Covetously

Thinking covetously entails thinking with jealousy about what others have achieved or the pleasures and material things they enjoy. It's marked by thoughts such as, "Look what they have? How did they do that? How can I get it for myself?" This type of thinking comes from attachment. We don't like that somebody else has things we don't have, whether it is success, a beautiful partner, a new car, a great job. It could be anything.

If we get into this state of mind, it is disturbing and can cause what I have referred to before as "stickiness of the mind." If we allow our minds to tell ourselves covetous stories, we tend to repeat them over and over again.

Perfectionism can also fall under the heading of covetousness. Perfectionism is one of the afflictions I have suffered with and still suffer, although not as much as in the past. It is covetous because we are coveting a state of perfection that we want but don't have and can't have. Even though there is no such thing as perfect, we're trying to outdo ourselves or outdo someone or some other measure of "perfect" that we hold as an objective pinnacle of perfection. It's being attached to an image of self or a set of circumstances that isn't real and not attainable if we see things as they are. Because of the impermanence of life, any perfect feeling or circumstance can and will change—possibly, in the next minute.

I know—I hear voices arguing that we should always try to perfect ourselves—but that is not right effort. We, of course, should try to be aware of where we can do better and where we have slipped into bad habits, but establishing a goal of perfection is not the way to do it. There is no perfection. What is perfect in this minute will be miserable in the next. Perfect would imply a fixed set of conditions. Here is perfect. Now is perfect. But the here and now becomes the there and then.

Thinking with Malice

Thinking with malice is thinking about how to harm someone, even—and more likely in our everyday lives—if the harm is verbal. Thinking, "If this person says or does something I don't like, I will get even by saying something that offends them or calls them out." We think about what we'll do or say the next time we see that person, and we regret that we didn't say something back to them when we first had the chance.

We can't get the malicious thought or the other person out of our heads. So much so, that the person becomes a caricature of themselves. The person becomes the "other" and we grasp so tightly at their "otherness" or "wrongness" that we aren't able to pause to see them as just like us, another person who is seeking the same happiness that we are but going about it in awkward ways sometimes.

Thinking with Antagonism

Thinking with antagonism can rise to the level of hostility or it can be a seething bitterness. We can slip into antagonistic thinking if we have a dislike of someone or some group and, instead of avoiding or ignoring the person or people, we actively oppose what they say or do. Frequently this takes place in our minds rather than appearing as outward behavior, but it is still antagonistic thinking.

In this mental scenario, we may find constant fault with the person or group of people and look for ways to criticize what they do or say. For example, when the person who causes this reaction in us does anything, even a self-improvement activity like going to the gym or beginning a volunteer activity, we may find a way to fault it and criticize it in our minds or outwardly. I hear this sort of criticism of others a lot. It's not a criticism of bad motives, but criticism of any motives, perspectives, or interests another might have.

Some people don't like sports and think that other people who do—people who watch football, soccer, hockey, or even my beloved baseball on television, or go to see a team play are wasting time. Thinking that it's stupid or a waste of time is a very antagonistic state of mind.

Or, someone else tries to help a homeless person by giving them money, and you think, "Oh, you're really stupid for doing that." If we spend time thinking about how other people are doing things that seem ignorant or irrational, we're not spending time investigating what we are doing, which is the only way we can help ourselves, anyone else, or the world.

The Practice of Right Effort

Right effort is directing our energy away from harmful, destructive trains of thought and toward the development of beneficial qualities. We just have to try without trying too hard and or not being too laid back either, but *just right*, like Goldilocks.

The key is to try. First, try to notice to find out what is happening. Notice when you typically do unskillful things, when you tend to do them. Think about what triggers you to do them then try to short-circuit or lessen the intensity of the triggers so you don't do them or don't do them as much.

A student asked his master, "What is the essence of the teachings, Master?" The master answered with one word: "Attention." So, the student asked again, "But beyond the essence, what is the whole of the teachings and how should I practice them?" And the master replied, "Attention, attention." So, the student tried one more time asking, "Can you offer another teaching to help me understand?" And the master replied, "Attention, attention, attention."

Paying attention to your thoughts and behavior, being on the look-out for unskillful habits, doesn't mean judging yourself. Don't be the judgmental GOD of you! Apply skillful means. Be like a gentle, kind parent with a small child. Don't grasp at the perfect or the failures. Just try. Then try again. And try again with your gentle parent encouraging you.

Pretty soon you will build one good habit and maybe rid yourself of one triggered behavior. Then, the trick is to maintain the behavior, which is the second part of the whole right effort thing.

This is such a good "everyday" practice. This isn't how to be some cave-dwelling monk or three-month retreatant. This is about doing something right now, then again later today, then tomorrow. It's a little habit, after a little habit, after another little habit. This is really what life is, isn't it? This "Everyday Buddhism" stuff is about doing the little things every day. It's not a holy attitude. It's an attitude of relaxing into your life, little by little, with a feeling of "everything is all right, right now."

That's what *really is* holy! Your life is holy. This life. This world. And your part in it. And so is your husband or wife, mother, the guy next door, and your annoying co-worker. And since it's all holy ground here, we should try to make it better for ourselves and the guy next door in any small way we can. Like the way we drive, or the way we wait in line, or the way we walk around the building at work, or the way we eat.

Doesn't all of this earn our respect? Our awareness and attention? Our caring and kindness? Isn't this what is holy? Isn't this what is sacred? There are a lot of things in each of our lives that could benefit from a little more awareness, attention, and caring, aren't there?

Because this attitude plays against—rather than with—our over-achievement, perfectionism, Protestant-work-ethic way of being in the world, it is more beneficial as a productive practice, as a spiritual practice. It's more about letting go of habits or the surrender of your false nature of self (as in "This is the way I do things" or "This is the way things should be done"), rather than achievement.

It's about being in whatever now is and being in it, in a balanced way. Because this type of effort, this practice of attention, as the Zen master says, is less about labor or effort, but more about your attention to what is happening in your life, in yourself, in your family, friends, and co-workers. When you really start to see how things are, you respond and live appropriately and in balance.

You might think Right Effort means practicing hard, but as I said earlier, it's not a driven practice. It's much more about the Middle Way, between extremes. Don't force yourself to endure meditation practices, or fitness practices, or nutrition, or study practices to exhaustion or frustration. If things become a chore, think again. Start again. Your practice should bring you joy. If it doesn't, then you may be bringing wrong view or wrong intention to your practice.

The Buddha taught that practice should be like a well-tuned string instrument. If the strings are too loose, they won't play a sound. If they are too tight, they will break. Practice should be nourishing, not draining.

Right Effort Practice: Adjust Your Habits

Typically, things aren't as hard as we imagine them to be. That's what "right" effort is all about. It's enough. Not too much; not too little. Just right. Right view plus intention and attention are all you need. What follows is a suggestion on how to apply right effort is an easy practice you can take up with "joyous effort."

Maybe list two or three things that you do—and wish you didn't or have regrets about doing—that you could try harder not to do and/or two or three things that you could try to incorporate in your life to make yourself and those around you happier.

It's about paying attention. It's about noticing. This is, in essence, right effort. This is the hard part. Adjusting your habits after noticing them isn't nearly as tough. Ask yourself where do you make too much effort or not enough? Where are you lazy or running on habit? Where are you too externally focused? Or too internally focused? It's about looking at yourself, the people and world outside of your head and noticing. Really notice. Pause your head stories and notice what's going on around you. Notice what you are doing.

Our habits have a powerful hold on us. We sleep-walk through our days with our habits in the lead. But once we try reducing or eliminating one bad habit or adding one good one and it works, it's empowering!

As an example, I will share my practice. First, I will list two things I will try to slowly eliminate, followed by two things I will try to do more of. Then it's your turn!

Two things I'm going to try to eliminate:

- Impatience with my family (spouse and dog) when I'm under time pressure or frustrations of feeling inadequate and unprepared. You will notice here that I've already taken the first big step of knowing my triggers: time constraints and frustrating feelings.

- Making quick judging comments about others, either silently or shared with others.

Two things I'm going to try to incorporate:

- When I feel driven or feel the tug of perfectionism, I will try to purposely take a walk around the yard or do a 10-minute meditation.

- I will try to always be conscious of listening more than speaking and try not to interrupt.

Reflection on Right Effort

Narrow Passage

Sometimes I struggle—twist and turn—
aiming at the narrow gap of me.
Drifting from shadows of steep conformity
a light appears, blazes through my brain,
engulfs my heart and uncovers my original self...

a vast conflicting wilderness of everything—
bad and good, stagnant brown and flowing blue,
desire and contentment,
choking grasses and a brilliant flame of maple leaves,
heaven and hell—

and nothing...

Life without force, not even emptiness
to steer for.

~ Wendy Shinyo Haylett

-7-

RIGHT MINDFULNESS & RIGHT CONCENTRATION

"When you give up your reactive checking,
Managing and goal-seeking—all of it—
There is a direct knowing, open and free.
Stop changing or altering it. Rest right there.

Then, when conceptual thinking arises,
Don't look at what arises: be what knows the arising.
Like an oak peg in hard ground,
Stand firm in awareness that knows,
And go deep into the mystery."

— Jigmé Lingpa, translation by Ken McLeod
in "A Trackless Path"
(From Jigmé Lingpa's "Revelations of Ever-present Good"
unfetteredmind.org/revelations-of-ever-present-good)

THE SEVENTH AND EIGHTH STEPS OF THE EIGHTFOLD PATH ARE RIGHT MINDFULNESS AND RIGHT MEDITATION. The Eightfold Path is "grouped" into three general areas: Wisdom teachings, Morality teachings, and Mental Discipline teachings. These are the last two of the Mental Discipline Teachings. Right Effort, discussed in the last chapter, is the first of three Mental Discipline teachings, followed by Right Mindfulness and Right Meditation.

I am referring to these two as Right Mindfulness and Right Concentration, but they are also referred to as Right Mindfulness and Right Meditation. I am approaching them together in one chapter because they are tied together under the now-culturally-familiar—or should I say "saturated"—concepts of mindfulness. They seem to be describing the same general activity of mind or mental discipline, but they are different. They are different, yet without one, you cannot know the other.

This is the key to Buddhist practice. It is my belief that the most important thing to know about Buddhism is that it teaches you the importance of—and joy in—being aware of what is.

Mindfulness is an openness of mind, allowing all mental and bodily experiences to be in mind; to be conscious of what you are doing—or to be aware—awareness. Mindfulness in this use, comes from the Pali word *sati* or the Sanskrit word *smriti*, meaning mindfulness, awareness, to be remembered, or retention.

Meditation or Concentration is a direction of thought and effort toward a single focus. It is derived from the Sanskrit *samadhi* which means to collect or bring together. This bringing together is why it is also referred to as Right Concentration. Yet, to complicate matters more, it is also associated with the word *samatha* or calm abiding, a term you may have heard in relation to a type of meditation. Applied to meditation, *samatha* and *samadhi* refer to a focused or "one-pointed" concentration with the intention of meditation.

An important point to help you distinguish the difference of relationship between concentration and mindfulness is to ask who or what directs the thought. Any being can concentrate, just watch a cat or a hawk focusing on their prey for hours on end. Right concentration is different because it is unified by intention, right intention.

When we concentrate with the combination of right intention and right effort, the horizon of our mind shifts. In more recent studies of neurotheology (which is a study of the identification of the biological basis of the religious experience—studying whether our minds create God or God created our minds to apprehend God), scientists discovered that Tibetan Buddhists and Franciscan nuns seemed to cease the activity of the parietal lobes in the upper back region of the brain during meditation and prayer. This region of the brain determines how we understand our body's position in space and where the self ends and non-self begins. This explains what many have experienced or described as the feeling of being on a higher plane during meditation and prayer.

I have experienced this during meditation, and I have talked with or read reports of others who have, too. So, it seems that meditation and prayer can dissolve the sense of separateness and, therefore, heighten a sense of interconnection. This only hints at the modifying effect, or change, that can take place when you meditate or pray. This is the intention we should hold when we practice mindfulness: To eliminate our sense of separation from others and from life as it is.

But how do we do it?

There is a story about the Buddha and a philosopher. The philosopher asked the Buddha to explain his practices toward the goal of enlightenment. The Buddha answered by saying: "We walk, we sit, we bathe, we eat." The philosopher responded much like we would respond to that answer: "Well, everyone does that. How is that special?" The Buddha answered, "We *know* we are walking, sitting, bathing or eating. Others don't."

Now, any of you who have tried meditation or tried to keep your mind on a single task—or keep your mind off a subject— knows how hard it is to direct thought. How many of you have driven home from work, reached your parking spot or driveway, and not have the foggiest remembrance of the ride home? Scary, huh?

This proves that we don't know what we're thinking or what's going on around us most of the time. We aren't mindful or aware, and we certainly aren't focused on what our thoughts are thinking, our emotions are feeling, and our bodies are experiencing unless it is an experience of pain in body or mind.

Mindfulness is really the starting point of Buddhist practice, because it teaches us to be aware of what "what is" is! Mindfulness, or awareness, is concerned with reality. It is clear seeing of what really is. This goes a long way to de-mystifying Buddhism, and it might also take away the mystique or romance for some. The Buddha did not teach enlightenment as an escape and meditation as the vehicle to transport your escape to another world. Nope, the Buddha taught that enlightenment is truly seeing and being in the life you are in. Think about the word "enlightenment." Enlightenment means to make something light, to shine a light on something or to make clear. He taught that enlightenment.

The Four Foundations of Mindfulness

The Buddha taught the principles of mindfulness in the "four foundations" from the Pali Canon. He explains the four foundations like this:

> *Here, monks, a monk abides contemplating body as body, ardent, clearly aware and mindful, having put aside hankering and fretting for the world; he abides contemplating feelings as feelings...; he abides contemplating mind as mind...; he abides contemplating mind-objects as mind-objects ardent, clearly awake and mindful, having put aside hankering and fretting for the world.*

The four foundations are being aware of our bodies, feelings, thoughts, and objects—as they occur, moment to moment. This is how the Buddha taught us to gain insight. And this insight will help us overcome our dissatisfaction. Don't get overwhelmed by the terms "insight", "insight meditation", "awareness", and others you might read or hear as you study Buddhism, mindfulness, or meditation. They are terms describing things we all already do. They are part of our nature. The Buddha teaches us how to be 100% in our nature without "hankering and fretting for the world." Insight simply means seeing things as they really are.

There is another popular story about an elderly grandmother coming to the Buddha asking how she could reach enlightenment if she couldn't renounce her family life. He told her that every time she went to draw water from the well to be aware of every single act, movement, and motion of her hands. He said that when she carried the water home in a jug on top of her head, that she be aware of every step of her feet; and when she did other chores, she should maintain continuous mindfulness and awareness of every moment, activity, and thought.

Sounds easy, but if anyone has ever tried this, in the spirit of Thich Nhat Hanh or other teachers' instructions, you know how hard it is. Yet, to me, this is where the sacredness of Buddhism lives. Being mindful of life is treasuring life, being grateful for everything in your life: all the things you can do, all the things you can see and hear and feel; and all the people, animals, and nature you share your life with. You can't help but see that sacredness when you pay attention.

Another story of the Buddha's teaching illustrates the power and sacredness of paying absolute attention to what is. One day the Buddha gathered his most realized disciples as if he was going to speak to them. Instead, he simply held up a flower. One of his disciples, Kasyapa, broke into a big smile and the Buddha commented, "Today only Kasyapa has understood my teaching." Kasyapa became the first patriarch of what has become the Zen lineage and that brief and wordless sermon of the Buddha is called the *Flower Sutra*.

It is our tendency to always look outside of ourselves for everything: for the answers to why things are the way they are and why they aren't. But we are looking with the conceptual mind. The mind that functions in duality. The mind that is looking "for" something. Not just looking at what is. But everywhere in the sacredness of our life, in nature surrounding us, are beautiful things. Bassho, one of the most famous Japanese poets wrote this haiku:

Look carefully.
The nazuna blooms
Along the fence—Ah!

The nazuna is a small wildflower that is easy not to see. That is life. Life is full of small flowers that we overlook in our non-awareness, non-mindfulness. The Zen teacher, Nansen, when asked what Buddhism is, answered, "everyday life."

That is one way to practice awareness or mindfulness, by taking the time to really experience what's around you, in your everyday life. And your everyday life includes **the four foundations of body, emotions, thoughts, and objects.**

Mindfulness of the Body

Mindfulness of body is done, primarily, by being mindful of our breathing. The Buddha advised going to the forest and sitting at the base of a tree. And for me, that is my preferred location. Not always literally, but with nature, even in my backyard or on a walk. But wherever we sit, if we find a quiet place and breathe— just breathe in and out mindfully, knowing but not controlling the breathing out and breathing in. Knowing but not controlling whether your breath is long or short. This is a deceptively simple practice. It sounds easy but it is remarkably tricky and equally profound.

As some of you are probably aware, no matter how committed and sincere you are, the mind has other plans. It will typically rebel and race off everywhere else but watching the breath. You will be confronted with distractions, memories, fantasies, plans, and fears. When I sit, all the things I need to do circle around and around in my mind, taunting me. You quickly realize you are not in control of your mind.

The other practice taught by the Buddha is to be aware of not just our breathing, but of our walking, standing, sitting, lying down—to know that we are doing those things.

The Buddha also taught us to reflect on our bodies' impurities and to separate and contemplate the four elements in our bodies: earth, water, fire, and air. Being aware of the elements helps us to understand that our bodies are made up of parts, components, or aggregates. There are five aggregates, or skandhas (in Sanskrit). They are form, or matter; sensation, or feeling; perception or cognition; mental formations, or mental habits, thoughts, ideas, opinions, compulsions; and consciousness. These are the things we mistakenly cling to as the self.

Mindfulness of Feelings & Mindfulness of Mind and Mind Objects

Contemplation or mindfulness of feelings is another good practice because feelings typically arise, take us over, get us to act—whether advisable or not—then go away. If we made a habit of just watching feelings, we would see how they rise up, wash over us, and vanish. They vanish all by themselves, we don't have to do anything. Yet if we cling to those feelings, we give them energy and a lifespan they don't naturally have.

Contemplation of the mind is to watch to see how your mind is disposed. The Buddha asked his monks to check their minds to see if there was lust, hate, confusion, distraction, concentration, or liberation. Again, the key here, too, is to just observe the mind states without judging them or identifying with them as me or mine, happy or sad, bad or good. The moment we identify with feelings and mental states is the moment we have become imprisoned by them.

Contemplation of "mind objects" is essentially a contemplation of things or the manifestations of reality. The four foundations teach us contemplation without grasping at anything in the world—or contemplation without conception.

How to Practice Mindfulness & Meditation

Impartial Watchfulness & Following the Breath

So how do we put these teachings into practice? We practice impartial watchfulness or bare attention to the present moment without conceptualization, elaboration, or comparison. We can remember to "pay attention" by using mindfulness bells. This is what Thich Nhat Hanh does at his retreat centers. Throughout the day mindfulness bells are sounded, reminding participants to stop and be aware of what is, in the present moment. Be aware of body, feelings, thoughts, and things. We can use any sound or activity in our daily life as mindfulness bells: a clock, phone, walking through a doorway, touching water, climbing stairs, stopping at red lights, or one of my teachers likes to encourage: going to the bathroom.

We use bells to check ourselves: Are we living, truly living in this moment? Or are we embroiled in a mental story of the past or future?

The breath is the perfect object for mindfulness focus. It is hard to conceptualize breath. You can't really breathe wrongly or rightly, you just breathe. I especially love Shunryu Suzuki's teaching on the breath in the book, *Zen Mind, Beginner's Mind*, as the "swinging door" for our interconnection with all beings. He says our "mind always follows our breathing."

When we inhale, the air comes into the inner world. When we exhale, the air goes out to the outer world. The inner world is limitless, and the outer world is also limitless. We say, "inner world" or "outer world" but there is just one world. What we call "I" is just a swinging door which moves when we inhale and when we exhale. It just moves. When your mind is pure and calm enough to follow this movement, there is nothing: no I, no world, no mind nor body; just a swinging door.

If you're walking in the woods, you're breathing together with the trees. The trees take our out-breath and we take their exhalations. We're breathing together. Mindful breathing is something that can be done anytime. It is the most natural quickie meditation. If you can't find time to meditate, do mindful breathing. It will calm your body, still your mind, and bring you immediately into the present, into what is.

You can also eat mindfully, brush your teeth mindfully, clean house mindfully, walk mindfully, watch your thoughts and feelings mindfully. You can focus your attention on a single object that is not the breath, like a mantra, koan, or deity visualization. It is all meditation.

Sitting Meditation

Then there is sitting meditation: *samatha*, or calming or concentration meditation, which can include *metta* practice or any single-pointed focus; *vipassana*, or insight meditation which can include movement and walking meditation. Samatha is said to be becoming absorbed into the object and *vipassana* is knowing the object. There is also analytical meditation that focuses on an analytical topic like the Four Thoughts that Turn the Mind to Dharma, the Four Noble Truths, or other topics; Zazen, meaning seated mind; and Tibetan or generalized visualization meditation practice.

Through meditation, we can see that we aren't our thoughts or feelings, yet we typically think we are. We become "abducted" by our thoughts and feelings, so much so that the mind sometimes seems a dangerous place to go alone. The trick is to be patient and kind with yourself when starting or continuing meditation. I think those of us in the West are particularly hard on ourselves, which is why I frequently hear people saying, "I just can't meditate!" Yet there is nothing difficult about it. It is, after all, "just sitting."

But when folks first start to meditate, they'll say, "But I have all these thoughts and feelings and aren't I supposed to stop my thoughts?" You can no more stop your thoughts then you can purposely stop breathing. However, when you begin to watch them, your thoughts will tend to perform for you, like two-year-old children or monkeys. Jumping about frantically, purposely trying to distract you. That's why they call it "monkey mind." Or you are plagued by bodily sensations: itches, hot, cold, pain. I admit I am frequently attacked by labels on clothes. We will get more into the things that hinder our meditation in the next section, as we examine The Five Hindrances to Meditation.

The Five Hindrdances to Meditation

There are hindrances to meditation and, as is typical of Buddhist thought, we have numbers for them. **The five hindrances to meditation are:**

- Desire

- Aversion

- Sloth

- Restlessness

- Doubt

I think these could be aptly applied to anything we try to do. Yet when we meditate, we more easily notice them because this is one time where we are really watching what we're thinking. Because we are watching our thoughts and feelings, we will be more likely to notice these hindrances. And when we do watch them, we see the demonstration of impermanence. Restlessness will arise, then it will fade away. Desire will arise and fade away. That's the beauty of impermanence, it is a self-correcting system—no effort needed on your part.

If you don't judge any of these hindrances as hindrances—or label them as anything else—you will remain in what meditation masters call "the view", "big mind", or Buddha Nature. This is the view that is beyond the distortion caused by judgment or conceptualization. It is the total clarity of things as they are, like a mirror. A mirror doesn't censor or conceptualize before reflecting; it reflects what is in front of it. Your mirror-like mind does the same thing, if not encouraged to conceptualize, judge, attach, or dismiss. Things will appear and disappear. Just like that.

In this respect, if you try to maintain that state of mind, whether you're meditating, working, eating, sleeping, working out, or whatever, your life becomes your practice.

You must continue to look inside to be able to see that you are nothing. As I have talked about and written before, the Tibetan word for Buddhist is *Nangpa* or "insider." It is only by looking inside that we will discover answers to any of our questions or solutions to any of our problems. It is only by seeing our thoughts clearly, and the actions they produce, that we can stop the causes of our own and others' suffering. It is said that when you stop all the causes of suffering and do it for the good of all beings, then you will reach enlightenment.

When we try to develop mindfulness, we are working to create a positive groove, a settling in, to create a habit of mind. And this takes time!

This is not about rocketing to the top, achieving or grabbing the brass ring of enlightenment! It is a slow process, letting mindfulness slowly diffuse through our mental processes, emotions, and physical behaviors until unwholesome mental states and emotions are derailed. Buddhism is not something we conquer, but something we work with—every day.

Awareness & The Many Forms of Meditation

Throughout my podcasts and this book, I have used the term "awareness" when talking about "non-judgmental awareness" and awareness without conceptual labels or emotionally charged stories. What is this awareness I refer to?

Merriam Webster defines awareness as "the quality or state of being aware: knowledge and understanding that something is happening or exists." The first part is a pretty good definition. After that, it sinks back into concepts with the words "knowledge" and "understanding." I like that it uses the phrase, "the state of being." So, when we are aware, we are in a state of being aware that something exists.

Let's play with these words a little. I like to do this as a trick to shake up my preconceived concepts of what things mean. According to the initial part of the definition, being aware is a state of being aware. It doesn't say a state of a self being aware of any specific thing, but a state of awareness. Awareness as being aware.

To play with this some more, let's go to the word "state." Again, referring to Merriam Webster, the word "state" is defined as a "mode or condition of being." We arrive back at the concept of being again. In playing with these words, what do we keep coming back to? A state of being. A state of being aware. Being aware of being aware.

And to push it further, I think you can stretch your mind to agree that since a subject or object isn't implied, except that something is happening or something exists, then let's define awareness as a state of being aware without the subject of who is being aware or who is being aware of what. You may think I'm just playing mind games. And maybe I am, but a good practice tip is to always question your assumptions, question your conceptualizations, and question subject and object.

Given the definition we just posited, how many times in our day do we think we are actually in a state of Be-ing, to begin with? Mostly we are in a state of think-ing or a state of plan-ning, even if we are Do-ing. Then there's the whole aware part. Being aware of something happening or that something exists. So, let's ask: Are we even aware of these things as they are happening? Or are we thinking about the last thing we did, or the next thing we are going to do, or planning what to say, or agonizing about what we didn't say?

Are we ever aware that we are just here experiencing awareness? Are we aware of our self in a state of awareness? Are we aware that someone else is over there, existing right with us? I'll answer these questions from my personal experience. It's rare when I am in a state Be-ing; when I am aware that I'm just here and being aware of things happening. Period. Do you know why that is? It's because I've been kidnapped.

Yep. Kidnapped and carried away by my thoughts. It's as if some sort of alien being slipped into my head and started dictating what I should do or feel. I should do this or that. I should feel this way or that way, and on and on. It's so noisy and demanding in these heads of ours that it's hard to be aware of our Be-ingness, our awareness.

I know we've talked about the importance of mindfulness and about meditation, but there is something else that is equally important to those trying to incorporate the 'tips and tricks' of Everyday Buddhism. And that is this awareness thing itself.

But, first, let's talk about the different types of meditation to help us establish a baseline of what mindfulness is and what awareness is.

Touring the Many Types of Meditation

There are so many meditation styles. One or more for everyone. But if you're new to meditation, don't let it overwhelm you. Just sitting is perfectly fine. Here are some general types followed by a listing of specific examples.

Focused Meditation

These are based on focusing on an object of meditation like breath, bodily sensations, mantra, visualization, or an outer object like a candle or picture of a guru or deity. This general type would include *samatha* or calm abiding, loving-kindness meditation, mantra meditation, sound meditation, kundalini, and especially breathing meditation like *pranayama.*

Insight / Open Focus Meditation

In this type of meditation, instead of focusing the attention on any one object, the focus is an open awareness of all aspects of our experience, without judgment or attachment. All perceptions, either internal (thoughts, feelings, memory, etc.) or external (sound, smell, sight, etc.) are acknowledged without engagement or reaction, in a moment-by-moment experience. Examples include mindfulness meditation, *vipassana*, and the Unified Mindfulness method I will share with you in the practice section.

Awareness Meditation

Awareness practices teach attention that is not focused on anything specific, but on awareness itself. It is also referred to as choiceless awareness, awake awareness, or pure being.

This effortless presence, or awareness of awareness, is actually the true purpose behind all kinds of meditation. All traditional techniques of meditation recognize that the object of focus, and even the process of mindfulness or monitoring, is a way to train the mind, so that effortless inner silence can be discovered but not grasped at. Eventually, both the object or focus of your meditation and the meditation process itself is left behind, and what's left is your true self or "pure presence."

In some techniques, this is the only focus from the beginning. Examples are the Self-Enquiry ("I am" meditation) of Ramana Maharishi, Tibetan *Dzogchen* and *Mahamudra*, some forms of Taoist Meditation, and some advanced forms of Raja Yoga.

This type of meditation is thought to require previous training to be effective, yet after my brief discussion of the different types of meditation, I propose that we can get a feeling for, or glimpse of, true "awareness" or "pure presence" just by practicing being aware as we go through our day.

There are many different meditation techniques based on different religious practices and no religions at all. At the risk of turning this chapter into a catalog, I will briefly discuss the different types of meditation I am aware of. There is a flavor for everyone.

Zazen

Zazen traces back to the Chinese Zen Buddhism (*Chan*) tradition and an Indian monk Bodhidharma (6th century CE). In the West, its most popular forms come from Dogen Zenji (1200–1253), the founder of Soto Zen movement in Japan.

Vipassana

Vipassana is a Pali word that means "insight" or "clear seeing." It is a traditional Buddhist practice, dating back to the 6th century BC. *Vipassana*, as taught in the last few decades, comes from the Theravada Buddhist tradition, and was popularized by S. N. Goenka and the *Vipassana* movement.

Mindfulness Meditation

Mindfulness meditation is an adaptation coming from traditional Buddhist meditation practices, especially *Vipassana*, but also having strong influence from other lineages (such as the Vietnamese Zen Buddhism of Thich Nhat Hanh). Mindfulness is the common western translation for the Buddhist term *sati*.

Mindfulness meditation was popularized in the West by John Kabat-Zinn. His Mindfulness-Based Stress Reduction program, developed in 1979, has been used in hospitals and health clinics.

Metta or Loving Kindness Meditation

Metta is a Pali word that means kindness and goodwill. This practice comes from the Theravada and Tibetan lineages. Compassion meditation has also become a popular study in contemporary science, demonstrating the efficacy of metta and related meditative practices.

Demonstrated benefits include strengthening the capacity to empathize with others; development of compassion, including a more loving attitude towards oneself; increased self-acceptance; greater feelings of competence about one's life; and increased feelings of purpose in life.

Mantra Meditation

A mantra is a syllable or word that is repeated for the purpose of focusing your mind. It is not an affirmation. Some meditation teachers insist that both the choice of word and its correct pronunciation are very important due to the "vibration" associated with the sound and meaning and for this reason, require initiation into the specific mantra practice. Others say that the mantra itself is only a tool to focus the mind and that the chosen word is completely irrelevant.

Mantras are used across Buddhist tradition (particularly Tibetan and Pure Land Buddhism) and in other traditions beyond Buddhism, including Hindu, Jainism, Sikhism, and Taoism.

Transcendental Meditation

Transcendental Meditation is a specific form of mantra meditation introduced by Maharishi Mahesh Yogi in 1955. In the late 1960s and early 1970s, the Maharishi achieved fame as the guru to the Beatles, The Beach Boys, and other celebrities while popularizing Transcendental Meditation.

Yoga Meditation

There are many different types of Yoga meditation taught in the yoga tradition. Yoga, meaning "union" goes as far back as 1700 B.C. and has as its highest goal spiritual purification and self-knowledge. Classical Yoga practice consists of rules of conduct, physical postures, breathing exercises (*pranayama*), and contemplative practices of meditation. Yet, most people today think of only the physical postures or physical practice.

The Yoga tradition is the oldest meditation tradition and also the one with the widest variety of practices, some of which are

Third Eye, *Chakra*, *Kundalini*, Sound or Nada Yoga, Tantra, and *Pranayama*.

Self-Enquiry

Self-enquiry is the English translation for the Sanskrit term *atma vichara*. It means to "investigate" our true nature, to find the answer to the "Who am I?" question, which culminates with the intimate knowledge of our true Self, our true being. We see references to this meditation in very old Indian texts, but it was popularized and expanded by the 20th-century Indian sage Ramana Maharshi (1879-1950).

The modern non-duality movement (or neo-advaita) is greatly inspired by the teachings of Ramana Maharshi. Many contemporary teachers employ this technique, the most famous ones being Mooji, who is a direct disciple of Sri Harilal Poonja, or Papaji, the renowned advaita master, and the teachers Adyashanti and Eckhart Tolle.

You may also have heard of this self-inquiry or Pure Awareness method as taught by Loch Kelly in his "Awake Awareness" teachings and in his book *Shift into Freedom* and also popularized by Sam Harris, the atheist philosopher, neuroscientist, author and podcast host of *Waking Up*.

Both Kelly and Harris were students of Tulku Urgyen Rinpoche, the Tibetan Kagyu and Nyingma lineage master who was renowned for his pointing-out instructions in *Dzogchen*.

Daoism/Taoism Meditation

Daoism/Taoism is a Chinese philosophy and religion emphasizing living in harmony with Nature, or Tao, and its main text is the Tao Te Ching, dating back to 6th century B.C. Later, some lineages of Taoism were also influenced by Buddhist meditation practices brought from India.

The chief characteristic of this type of meditation is the generation, transformation, and circulation of inner energy. The purpose is to quiet the body and mind, unify body and spirit, and harmonize with the Tao. Some styles of Taoist meditation are specifically focused on improving health and giving longevity.

Qigong

Qigong is a Chinese word that means "life energy cultivation." It is a body-mind exercise for health, meditation, and martial arts training. It typically involves slow body movement, inner focus, and regulated breathing. Traditionally, it was practiced and taught in secrecy in the Chinese Buddhist, Taoist, and Confucianist traditions. Today it emphasizes the use of concentration exercises and the circulation of energy.

Christian Meditation

The goal of Christian contemplative practices is a combination of a deeper understanding of the Bible and a closer intimacy with God/Christ. Some forms are contemplative prayer, which usually involves the silent repetition of sacred words or sentences, with focus and devotion. *Lectio Divina*, a type of contemplative reading and simply contemplation comes from a monastic tradition and it is focused on a personal immersion (versus thinking) into the teachings and events in the Bible. A simple sitting with God or contemplative prayer is a silent meditation usually preceded by contemplation or reading, with a focus of mind, heart, and soul on the presence of God

Sufi Meditation

Sufism is the esoteric path within Islam, where the goal is to purify oneself and achieve mystical union with the Supreme, or *Allah*. The practitioners of Sufism are called Sufis, and they follow a variety of spiritual practices, many of which were influenced by the tradition of Yoga in India. Their main techniques include contemplation of God (*muraqabah*); Sufi mantra meditation (*zikr*, *jikr*, or *dhikr*); heartbeat meditation; Sufi breathing meditation; Bond of love meditation; gazing meditation; Sufi walking meditation; and Sufi whirling.

Guided Meditation

Guided meditation is a modern approach. It is an easier way for a beginner to start a meditation practice since you can find many guided meditations based on several of the traditions previously mentioned in smartphone and computer applications, YouTube, and on websites of specific traditions and teachers. Guided meditation can be a good way to introduce a practice, but it is recommended that once you get the hang of it and wish to take your practice to the next level, you try meditation unassisted by audio and apps.

You can find many different styles of guided meditations including traditional meditations with the voice of the teacher illustrating or guiding your attention to a meditative state. Examples are the ones offered by Thich Nhat Hanh and Tara Brach.

Guided imagery meditation makes use of imagination and visualization, guiding the imagination of an object, entity, scenery or journey. The purpose is usually healing or relaxation. Relaxation and body scans help achieve deep body relaxation. These meditations are usually accompanied by soothing instrumental music or nature sounds.

Affirmation Meditation

Affirmation-style meditations are usually coupled with relaxation and guided imagery with the purpose of imprinting a message or suggestion in your mind.

Binaural Beats

Binaural Beats were originally discovered in 1839 by physicist Heinrich Wilhelm Dove. He discovered that when signals of two different frequencies are separated, one to each ear, your brain detects the variation and tries to reconcile the difference, shifting brain waves to either Delta, Theta, Alpha or Beta waves, depending on the frequency. The altered brain waves then help in producing states of relaxation, sleepiness, focus or concentration, meditation, creativity, and relief of anxiety.

Arriving at Awareness

Now that we've toured the many ways to meditate, let's do a deeper exploration into awareness. I won't go into all the different types of awareness or Pure Presence teachings and teachers. There are so many, including those I mentioned earlier, like Mooji, Adyashanti, Eckhart Tolle, and Loch Kelly. They have emerged from different traditions and teaching styles, including the modern non-duality or *advaita* movement, Tibetan *Dzogchen* and *Mahamudra* traditions, and the self-enquiry method of Bhagavan Sri Ramana Maharshi. With this form of meditation becoming so popular, it would not be difficult to connect with teachings through books, websites, audio CDs, podcasts, or meditation apps.

As I talked about earlier in this chapter, how many times in a day are we truly aware? Or maybe I should be more precise and say how many times are we truly aware of being aware? That is really the heart of the matter.

Awareness is simply that. It doesn't have to be aware of some thing. Our minds are aware by their very nature, yet that nature is obscured by thoughts and emotions like the clear blue sky is obscured by clouds. Sometimes the clouds are white puffy clouds and sometimes they are dark and angry. We normally don't judge or conceptualize the clouds, unless we are planning an outside event or are a weather buff, and we have confidence that the clear blue sky is there behind them. However, we are generally not aware of the clear mind of natural awareness because we've been kidnapped by a train of thoughts and the emotions they kick-off.

Getting to know awareness is easier if we first practice meditation with an object, like the breath, or mantra, or gazing at a candle. When we are meditating on the object and we become aware that we lost the object of meditation in a journey on the train of thoughts, at that moment we have become aware, as long as we don't judge or criticize ourselves for letting thoughts carry us away.

That's why, when I'm working with a coaching client in the practice of mindfulness or meditation, I tell them that when they become aware that they are lost in thought, it is a huge success and something to celebrate in the practice of meditation. If they can notice it—be aware of it without judgment—they have successfully experienced a moment of clear awareness.

That clear awareness can be the object of meditation. It exists between our thoughts. It exists underneath our emotions. And, if we are meditating on the arising and passing away of thoughts and emotions, I encourage you to look for it. Look for it, but don't chase away thoughts or judge thoughts as getting in the way. Just quietly observe the arising and passing away of thoughts and be aware of that space in between. If you look back—look in—you'll spot it. You may only notice it for a few seconds before you will be kidnapped by another thought or emotion, but don't beat yourself up. You will notice it and you will be aware of noticing awareness again.

Our problem tends to be that we try *too* hard. We grasp at being a "meditator." We cling to doing it right, trying not to think and, as soon as we do that, we've put a death grip on the relaxed and spacious awareness that is our minds' natural way of being. And if we tend to think the opposite, of going into our meditation practice with the goal of "chilling" or being calm, then we are more likely to drift away in a daydream, allowing the thought train to kidnap us until we are a million miles away.

To catch a glimpse of awareness, it's best to be like Goldilocks looking for a space that's not too hard or not too soft. Or, as the story goes, the Buddha taught that the method for meditating properly is like that of getting the perfect sound out of a stringed instrument, with the strings not too tight or not too loose. Our mental attitude around awareness and meditation should not be too concentrated or too relaxed.

A good way to investigate this for yourself is to think of moments in your life where you have experienced—even briefly—a sense of being aware of yourself in life, as part of life, part of the experience, while not feeling yourself in the awareness.

There are few times in life where I have been aware of myself in life, as life. Some people refer to them as peak experiences or moments of insights—a glimpse of everything as perfection and me as a part of that perfection. But they have been far too rare and only glimpses. It is only relatively recently that I have been able to experience those moments by seeking after them using a meditative awareness practice.

Typically, the way I have been able to experience moments of awareness in my meditation practice is to start with my typical meditation practice, which is using the "See-Hear-Feel" practice technique from the Unified Mindfulness approach, which I will share in the practice section of this chapter. In this practice, I use an object of focus as part of the meditation, such as a sight, sound, or an internal or external feeling. My typical object of focus is either "Hear-Out" using external sounds as my object of focus, or more of a "Do-Nothing" approach added to the See-Hear-Feel technique, which makes it like an "awareness and "just-sitting" hybrid.

After I've been stable in that and I've opened my space and allowed thoughts to come and go without chasing, I turn my awareness of sound, or "hear out" around. I use a technique taught by Loch Kelly where I note that I am hearing and turn my awareness back around at myself and ask, "Who is Hearing?" At that point, my awareness will typically "unhook", as Loch Kelly refers to it, from the thinking area inside my forehead and shift down, either to my heart or outside of myself, somewhere behind my head. At that point, I become aware of spacious awareness that isn't hooked or anchored to my self.

Before I started actively practicing this, I merely found myself in an experience of spacious awareness. I hope that my relating these experiences will help you connect with the experiences you have had of being in awareness or being aware of a subject-less and object-less open awareness of your experience. Your state of being aware. As a child, those peak experiences came while walking in the woods or just sitting with my back against a tree, watching a squirrel. As an adult, I remember three vivid examples of these divine portals beyond feelings, perceptions, impulses, and words.

One occurred on a late September afternoon, I was standing on the deck of a friend's condominium built into the side of a steep hill overlooking Canandaigua Lake, one of the Finger Lakes. While my hosts and other guests went into the condo, taking with them their happy leaf-peeping party chatter, I remained, watching a lone tern ride drafts against a dark, cloudy sky. That was all. But time stopped, thoughts stopped, my sense of self stopped, as I seemingly became a part of the tern, the golden and red trees on the hill, the sun, and the clouds. I was exhilarated by an immense joy beyond reason or cause. I wanted to describe it to my companions when I joined them again but had no words.

Three other experiences happened in less poetic settings.

Once, while watching our Labrador and German Shepard-mix dog, Ayla, contentedly chewing her chew toy, my awareness expanded beyond myself as me. Watching her chew, I seemed to become both her chewing, the chewing, and the me that I didn't identify with, but was aware of.

And, one day, I glanced out the window near my desk, taking a break from my work and computer screen and noticed my elderly neighbor brushing the snow from his car. I watched for a few minutes that seemed like hours. Nothing happened that I hadn't seen a million times before, but his slow, attentive, careful, and caring snow brushing penetrated my heart with a simple yet brilliant love for my neighbor, myself, everyone, and everything.

Another time where I experienced the grace of a peek into the perfection of everything was while lying in bed, ill, and in pain. I had been ill for some time. I was exhausted and depressed by the pain and the lack of promise for a quick resolution. For some reason, I was able to truly relax "into" the pain, depression, and fear. I was able to be in it, as an experience alone—not characterized as bad, or pain, or suffering. At that precise moment, I wasn't me. For a moment between the rushing screams of thoughts of pain coming from everywhere, there was no me—but there I was, and I knew that I was.

Some might describe these experiences as described in the Bible, in *Philippians* 4:7: "And the peace of God, which passeth all understanding, shall keep your hearts and minds through Christ Jesus."

The Indian poet, Rabindranath Tagore, was watching the sunrise in a Calcutta street when he wrote, "suddenly, in a moment, a veil seemed to be lifted from my eyes.... There was nothing and no one whom I did not love at that moment."

Right Mindfulness Practice: Unified Mindfulness

I referred to the Unified Mindfulness approach to meditation earlier in this chapter. **This system of meditation helps strengthen your concentration power, sensory clarity, and equanimity.**

Concentration power is the ability of selective attention.

Sensory clarity is the ability to clearly distinguish visual, auditory, and bodily sensations from each other, separating the threads of experience. It is also the ability to note when a sensory event arises and note when it passes.

Equanimity is the ability to remain calm and non-reactive despite the situation or experience. It is strengthened by the wisdom of knowing nothing is permanent in life and things come and they go. Despite it sometimes being considered as aloofness or coolness, it is much more of a warm acceptance of life. It is the ability to overcome the instinct to grasp and cling.

The Unified Mindfulness meditation system strengthens these three powers through a method of meditation that can best be described as a unification of *samatha* or calm abiding and *vipassana* or insight meditation. The method is built on a See-Hear-Feel practice.

See-Hear-Feel Practice is the noticing where your attention is focused based on three sensory categories.

- See includes what you see in your environment and also what you see in your imagination.

- Hear includes what you hear in your environment and also what you hear in your mind, like talking to yourself or hearing a tune stuck in your head.

- Feel includes physical sensations and emotional feelings.

A quick introduction to the practice is to notice where your attention goes from moment to moment. Keep your attention on what you notice for a few seconds then move to the next experience you notice. Decide whether what you're noticing is "see", "hear", or "feel." If you're not sure what category, go ahead and guess. If you notice more than one, just pick one to focus on. And if you notice too many at once and miss labeling some, that's fine, too.

Once you identify the category, label it by saying out loud or to yourself, "see" or "hear" or "feel". If you notice the same experience twice, it's fine to repeat the label. Keep a steady pace and even tone when you label what you're noticing.

The key to this practice is that it's easy to do, it works with what's around you at any moment, and you can do the practice at any time. When you engage in this practice, you will find your concentration and sensory clarity does improve rapidly. And if you practice long enough you will notice the feeling of equanimity.

This is just an introduction. To discover more about this practice, you can take their free core training, which you can find out more about here: https://unifiedmindfulness.com/core.

Reflection on Right Mindfulness & Concentration

The Purelands

Somewhere beyond the fence,
or before,
a vast space that can't be contained by fences
arises
in a glimpse
of your own light—

lacking nothing
being everything:
rotted wood, a crystalline sky,
bent nails, a field mouse, jeweled grasses
and the hoax of self—

reflected perfectly
in your heart mind—
mirror of infinite light
radiant and perfect—
from the spaciousness
between your thoughts.

~ Wendy Shinyo Haylett

PART FOUR: ACTION • PRACTICES & REFLECTIONS

-8-

SUMMARY OF PRACTICES & REFLECTIONS

You Gotta Try It To See If It Works

*"We don't receive wisdom; we must discover it
for ourselves after a journey no one
can take for us or spare us."*

— *Marcel Proust*

I RECORDED AND RELEASED A PODCAST EPISODE (EPISODE 4) CALLED "WHAT DOES BUDDHISM SAY ABOUT....?" AS A FUN WAY OF EMPHASIZING A COUPLE OF THINGS:

One, that depending on any external person, group, or belief system to give you the answers to everything is, well, a little crazy, yet that's what we seem to do. And the problem with that is it prevents us from sitting with the questions.

And, two, having questions without answers is OK.

We live in a world with instant answers to everything. We can Google anything and everything we have a question about and find the answer. It's great. But we're completely alien to the practice of reflecting. When we have a problem or question, we look for an immediate answer. And we look out there; we look externally. We look on our smartphones or computers, on Google or Wikipedia, and on Facebook. Then we text our friends and if they don't have a quick text response, we feel a little panicked because we've exhausted our external sources. It's rare that we would even think to sit down for reflection.

Some of you may remember *The Andy Griffith Show* that was popular in the 1960s. When Sheriff Andy had a question or a problem he sat out on his front porch to think. Have you ever pulled yourself away for a minute to think? Personally, I've been trying to break the habit of picking up my phone to Google something I have a question about. Sometimes I catch myself googling the most ridiculous little thought just because I'm curious. There is nothing wrong with curiosity, but the habit of looking externally for an answer—or even looking for an answer at all—hijacks the mind from reflection and steals the experience of stewing in the question. When you stew in a question, even if you don't arrive at an answer, the question changes and transforms you. Your reactivity lessens and what was once a question becomes part of the experience of what is.

The podcast episode I referred to a few paragraphs ago was inspired by one of my favorite podcasts, *The Dharma Realm*, with the Rev. Harry Bridge, of the Buddhist Church of Oakland, and Scott Mitchell, the Dean of Student and Faculty Affairs at the Institute of Buddhist Studies. I stole the concept of the "Buddhist Answer to Everything" from their February 23, 2019 podcast titled "The Buddhist Answer for Everything."

I changed what they did up by actually giving an answer.

Have you ever seen that Liberty Mutual commercial with two young guys stuck on the side of the road with a flat tire? One of the guys is on the phone with his dad holding some sort of tool that is clearly not a lug wrench and says, "Don't worry, Dad, I know what a lug wrench is!" ... and then he looks to the other guy and whispers, "Is this a lug wrench?"

The other guy looks a little confused then clearly shakes his head "yes" and says: "Maybe", in a really good bit of acting that cracks me up every time I see it.

And that is my Buddhist answer to everything: "Maybe."

"Maybe" is a great word to use as a mantra in daily life. It can short-circuit reaction and replace it with reflection. Things happen. Immediate answers or reaction to what happens—

questions, insults, anger—is not required. If we keep as our intention a calm, non-harming state of mind, a "maybe" response can slow everything down.

The Buddhist answer to everything has something to do with intention. Since, generally, we don't really know others' intentions and, most of the time, we are barely acquainted with our own, "maybe" seems like a good answer.

Intention is one of the conditions that contribute to the way things are. Things are not what they seem because "things" as such—all things that we think are real and grab on to as a fixed, never-changing thing—are not the kind of real we think they are. I mentioned before the loose quote from *The Lankavatara Sutra*: "Things are not what they seem; nor are they otherwise." This is saying that things are as we label them, and we label them as we perceive them at the moment. But someone else may perceive them in a different way and we, also, may perceive them in a different way at a different time, under different circumstances.

Yep, that's a maybe. The other Buddhist answer to everything could be "it depends."

I got the idea for that podcast from all the times someone asks me directly, or asks indirectly in a Facebook post on some group I belong to, or asks on the Reddit website, something like "What does Buddhism say about _____?" Fill in the blank. Or "Are all Buddhist vegans?"

Generally, it's about some social, cultural, or political hot-button issue, like what does Buddhism say about abortion? Or what did the Buddha say about same-sex marriage? Or smoking marijuana? Or questions like that. I always want to answer, "it depends." But I can't really say that, because I don't want someone to feel like I'm being sarcastic or making fun of them and their question.

It's a real problem to answer for all of Buddhism and it's even harder to answer the questions that start with "What did the Buddha say about?" I have the same trouble with those "What would the Buddha do?" and "What would Jesus do?" questions in articles and blog posts. I know they mean well and are trying to offer sound advice about the best way to react to situations in this confusing world, but it seems a profound over-simplification of the Dharma and those trying to live according to the teachings of Jesus.

I will only speak for the Buddhist side of things, though.

Of course, the Buddha, like Jesus, cannot be quoted like people alive today, with word-for-word transcripts from a recording. What can be attributed to the Buddha is from the Pali Canon or the teachings of the "three baskets." One of which are teachings directed to monks and nuns, others are his sutras or discourses, and the third are the more philosophical summaries thought to be classified by scholars.

But all of these were put together after the Buddha's death, even though it is widely accepted that his sutras and his rules for monks and nuns were committed to memory by his close followers. The words of Jesus are also written by others after his death, as well.

This makes it difficult to be sure what the Buddha actually said some 2,500 years ago, let alone a bit sketchy to proclaim that any of it directly addresses any of the political or ethical questions someone has today.

But you wouldn't know that by glancing at social media. The "Buddha" may be the most quoted person on social media. Unfortunately, most of the quotes I see attributed to the Buddha—written in fancy fonts over beautiful, scenic photographs—have little or nothing to do with what the Buddha is recorded to have said. And they generally don't align with the main tenets of the teachings of the Buddha.

I'm all for spreading positive messages to drown out the drumbeat of the doom and sky-is-falling messaging that overwhelms us today, but just because it sounds nice and positive isn't verification that it was something the Buddha said or something that is a principle of Buddhist practice.

There is a website dedicated to debunking most of these: https://fakebuddhaquotes.com/. On that website, they even suggest that there is some truth to some. I have suggested more people get used to checking it before posting a Buddha quote, much like they've gotten used to checking Snopes, the urban legend debunking site.

One of the quotes they highlighted on the site is one I actually saw on my Facebook feed. It is: "Love is a gift of one's innermost soul to another so both can be whole." I had a little talk with this post, trying to calm myself down. I was tempted to comment but, thankfully, thought again. Just the mere fact that "innermost soul" was used should have been a tip-off that this couldn't be a real quote from the Buddha. I don't think the Buddha referenced an "innermost soul" at any time. The Buddha remained silent on many of the big questions asked of him. Some of which are recorded to be are the self and the universe eternal? And will Buddha's self exist after death?

We've already talked quite a bit about the discrete existence of self and things, enough to know that the Buddha couldn't answer this question with the questioner's hoped-for definitive yes or no answer. Because nothing is definitive, right? To question whether self or things are eternal or infinite is like asking if the horns of a rabbit or the lips of a chicken are eternal or finite.

If the Buddha said you were or he was eternal, then the questioners would grasp at everything being real and existing forever, and it would increase their suffering. If he tried to answer in the detail needed to explain what he was enlightened to, then he would feel that his audience, his questioner, might not understand or would misunderstand. So, the most skillful means would be not to answer the question.

Or another skillful answer for today could be my answer, "Maybe."

The Buddha taught for 40 or 50 years from his enlightenment to his death and the way he taught was by taking answers to individual questions. This meant that some of the teachings of the Buddha over the decades contain what appear to be conflicting answers. This is because he gave answers to individual people, based on what they needed at the time and based on their level of understanding. The Buddha did not stand and proclaim doctrine, but he counseled instead.

As I mentioned earlier, the closest we have to the canonization of the Buddha's teachings is the Pali Canon that was put together after his death. And there is some debate that there are recorded teachings of the Buddha from even earlier than that. So there really isn't a single "dogma" that explains the teachings of Buddhism.

And there really isn't a single "Buddhism" or "Buddhists" that all practice the same thing. There many different "Buddhisms" over the multiple traditions, schools, and lineages across the globe. And each of these has different teachings and practices. And, no, we aren't all caricatures of grinning, vegan, pacifist liberals who practice meditation.

Buddhism is conceptual and experiential. It doesn't have a singular ruling body, organization, dogma, or authority. And, no, the Dalai Lama is not the head of "Buddhism", like the Pope.

So, what does all this have to do with the fourth part of this book and its focus on action? Hint: It has to do with the heading of this introductory section, "You Gotta Try It to See if It Works." The key here is that Buddhism is all about practice. The Buddha-Dharma is experiential. You need to find the answers for yourself. You need to apply what you read and learn to understand it. I can't speak for Buddhists. I can only speak for me and for my understanding and practice of the Dharma.

I think most of the time when people ask what Buddhism says or questions you on your expression of Buddhism, they're looking to justify their own position on something, like not eating meat.

If you are seeking reassurance that what you believe is right, maybe you should look inside, instead of outside for some authority to back you up. You should look to see if the opposite of what you believe is also true. Which brings us back to "Maybe", doesn't it? "Maybe" puts certainty on hold. Giving you time to find your own truth or find that another's truth is also true?

The Buddhist path that I follow is one where I ask my own questions while looking for the answers, with an openness and expectation that there may not be any definitive answers. For me, the practice of Buddhism is about getting comfortable with uncertainty and sitting with my questions.

That's why the path of Everyday Buddhism I outline in this book is Awareness, Acceptance, Appreciation, and Action. It is the structure the Buddha taught in the Four Noble Truths:

- **Awareness** of the discontent that is part of life.

- **Acceptance** that discontent is part of life and that when trying to grasp at something other than what is, you feel suffering.

- **Appreciation** for things as they are is the equanimity that arises when not clinging or pushing away.

- **Action,** or establishing a practice of awareness, acceptance, and appreciation through the practice of the Eightfold Path. This is the action needed to free your life from the suffering brought on from fighting life as it is.

Right View Practice: No-Self & Emptiness

I will offer two small practices (actually, thoughts to play with) so that you can try to directly experience emptiness and emptiness of self. I say "try" because although Buddhas and many great Dzogchen or Mahamudra masters experience and continue to experience emptiness—have gone beyond and live in sunyata—I have only glimpsed it. Yet, in the trying, I get closer and closer to living in and from a place where concepts don't keep me anchored. And when not anchored to concepts, freedom emerges and offers the space of just living and experiencing, just being, and being aware of just being.

Nagarjuna, the Indian Mahayana philosopher said, "All is possible when emptiness is possible. Nothing is possible when emptiness is impossible." This is the "good news" of Buddhism.

Nagarjuna also posited the concepts of the Two Truths. I've written earlier about the problem with the word "truth" and the doctrine of Two Truths makes this even more apparent. The Two Truths are the ultimate truth and conventional truth. Ultimate truth is that everything is empty of being a discrete, permanent thing because everything is interdependent, everything is co-arising. This means that all things and all experiences arise dependently, not by their own power, but dependent on conditions that lead to their coming into existence.

Conventional truth is the truth of things in our everyday, walking-around existence. The truth of a table or a chair. We accept the table is there and it exists, but as we've discussed using the concept of emptiness, the table is a thing only because of its parts. It's empty of a "table essence." If you look for a table essence, or its inherent existence, you will find that it is dependent on the wood it is made of, the carpenter or factory worker who created it, the tree that the wood came from, and on and on.

The same is true of our self. We cannot point to one, discrete permanent self as our self. The body changes, the mind changes, our roles in interacting with others change. Which is the self? Conventional truth tries to define things as what they seem to be. But what is big? What is small? That depends on putting the big thing next to another thing and seeing if it is bigger. So, the big thing depends on something else for its "bigness". It is dependent.

And the other thought to play with, in your practice of emptiness, is to ask what makes one object what it is, as compared to another? What makes it what it is, as you label it? What is its essence?

Look around the room. Are the door and window the same? They both have a rectangular pane of glass. Are the grey squirrel and the chipmunk the same? They both have a bushy tail. What is the "doorness" of the door, the "windowness" of the window, the "squirrelness" of the squirrel, or the "chipmunkness" of the chipmunk?

Let your mind play with this concept. You may end up not being so sure of all the labels you put on everything.

Now, let's do the same thing with your concept of self. Try to find a picture of yourself when you were around two or three years old. Stare at the picture for a while. Do you feel as if you are looking at you? Do you feel yourself in that picture? Conventionally, you know that was you at that age. You remember how you looked from looking at pictures of yourself at that age.

Now, look at yourself in the mirror. Which one is you? The person in the photo or the person in the mirror? Are they both you? How can that be? You were the you in the picture at that time and you are the you in the mirror now. But both "yous" are dependent on something, right? Dependent on change. Dependent on time. When you were three you had blonde hair. Now you have grey hair. If your hair color is a concept you use to describe yourself and the color you use as a description of yourself is blonde, then you must not be you now, because you aren't blonde.

It's all very shaky, isn't it? The caution here is not to get stuck in thinking from the point of absolute truth or the point of conventional truth. These concepts are keys to seeing reality as it is. Thinking that things are permanent is incorrect but getting stuck in the concept of impermanence is not a good way to think either because it can foster a nihilistic view of life. This is what is meant by the middle way.

It is not that we don't have a self and things don't exist, but we don't exist, and things don't exist in the way we think they do. When you explore these concepts, you are entering into an expanded understanding of life as it is, which prevents you from clinging to seeing life as you would like it to be or that someone tells you it is. If you explore these thoughts deeply it is a form of meditation, analytical meditation, which can help lead you to longer and longer glimpses into *sunyata*.

The types of meditative practices I just illustrated can help loosen your mental grip on the rigid concepts of the way things are and, instead, allow you to freely experience things as they are, as experience arises and co-creates your reality with you.

Reflection on Right View

Essence of Light

Sun slips from behind ignorance
illuminating illusion,
but try to find it with your eyes
point even to its shadow,
with wisdom hidden
under your clothes,
inside your name.
But doing nothing,
being nothing,
a sage awakens darkness
penetrates the essence of light.

~ Wendy Shinyo Haylett

Right Intention Practice: Intention + Action

Three key concepts emerged in this chapter on right intention: a big story, meaning, or purpose; the intention to do something or try to do something aligned with the big story or purpose; and completing the intention through action. Intention in Buddhism is all of those things. Action without intention can easily be misguided, habitual, or worse. Intention without action is wishful thinking.

In Buddhism, to create the force of karma we need intent combined with deeds or action. Good intent plus good deeds contribute to good karma. Bad intent and bad deeds contribute to bad karma. Our legal system uses similar criteria. It is not enough to have committed an illegal act, but the intent to commit the act must also be proved to establish guilt and determine the type of sentencing.

Don't freak out about my mention of karma. You do not have to subscribe to a belief in rebirth to understand and accept the workings of karma. Karma is, essentially, the consequences of actions and intentions.

But which is more important? Actions or intentions? Without thinking too deeply, I believe most of you would answer actions. And many times in this book I stress the importance of acting on our intentions, since intention alone is only a wish. Yet, without the proper or right intention, action is reaction. A practice of purposeful intention can condition us to carry out actions that we wish to carry out. No empty wishes unfulfilled and no regrets over-reactions not intended.

We can take vows that keep our hearts and heads aligned with how we would like to act or the type of person we would like to become or something less formal like establishing a daily practice that aligns our thinking with our true intentions. So, rather than rushing out the door to work with the news blaring or responding to a Facebook post with coffee in hand, maybe there is more we can do?

What are some of the ways you can think of to reinforce your good intentions? What practices or habits could help you spread good intentions through the world?

My suggestion for a right intention practice is to adopt and build a habit of "Everyday Gassho", a practice created by Rev. Koyo Kubose, my Sensei with the Bright Dawn Center of Oneness Buddhism. I began this practice in 2012 as part of a commitment to completing the 21-Day Daily Dharma Program. When a Bright Dawn lay minster colleague and friend suggested I begin this practice to start incorporating more spiritual ritual in my life, I scoffed a bit at how simple it seemed. Yet, I began the Everyday Gassho practice, completed the 21 days, and I am still doing it today. I discovered it was anything but simple in building a habit and establishing a practice that joined a big intention with a small, daily action.

This simple practice became a powerful part of my life. I attribute that power to the combination of a purpose or intention bigger than myself with the fulfilling of it in a planned or habitual action, even a seemingly small action. Will my two daily gasshos lead to world peace or saving the planet? Probably not directly, but they will keep me aligned with my own good intentions and bigger purpose, which should help make me a better person every day. I believe it can do the same for you.

The Everyday Gassho practice and an article on "Why Gassho", written by Rev. Koyo Kubose, is included below:

Everyday Gassho Introduction

The act of Gassho is done by putting the palms of your hands together in front of your heart and bowing your head. Gassho may be done sitting or standing, with eyes closed or open, and with or without meditation beads. As part of the 21-Day Program, a Harmony Gassho and Gratitude Gassho are done daily in front of your home altar or Special Place of Tranquility, also known as SPOT.

Harmony Gassho

The Harmony Gassho is done in the morning and sets your motivation for the day. Choose a time when it will best fit into the flow of your usual morning routine. If helpful, post a "Gassho" reminder sign in a visible place. One suggestion is to do your morning Harmony Gassho just before breakfast. As an aid to making Gassho a habit, you can mentally make eating breakfast contingent upon first doing Gassho. No Gassho, no meal. Keep a planner, calendar, or app to record the completion of your morning Harmony Gassho.

The verbal recitation accompanying your morning Gassho can be the word "harmony." In lieu of any other strong considerations, it is suggested you use the recitation "harmony" during your initial 21-Day Program. Other recitations can be introduced later. Your recitation can be spoken with any degree of loudness or simply be said to yourself. The depth or power of the recitation is facilitated through your breath. After a moderately deep (but not overly long) inhalation through your nose, make your recitation as you exhale through your mouth. The sound of the last syllable should be extended until the end of the exhalation. As an approximate guideline, your inhalation can be about 3-5 seconds long, whereas your exhalation should be about 9-15 seconds long. Keep your body and head erect as you inhale. As the last syllable of the recitation is finished, slowly bow your head, keeping your hands and body still. At the end of the recitation, most people like to stay in the finishing position for a while (perhaps for 1-3 normal breaths) so that you don't get the feeling of rushing off immediately after the recitation.

The preceding is a description of a standard or basic procedure; other variations can be developed later after the initial 21-day period. Other than doing the one recitation, there isn't a recommended number of additional recitations you should do. More is not necessarily better but if desired, you can do more than one (although it probably is not a good idea to do more than three at a given time).

The underlying sentiment of the Harmony Gassho is that you will try your best to have a spirit of cooperation with others, and always be as calm and patient as possible. The seed of this sentiment will gradually blossom into an understanding that can be called wisdom.

Gratitude Gassho

The Gratitude Gassho is done in the evening and recaps your day. It is suggested that you do it just before eating dinner, again mentally making eating contingent upon first doing Gassho. On days you eat out, you can do your Gratitude Gassho just before going to bed. Perhaps a "Gassho" reminder note near your bed would be helpful. Immediately after doing your Gratitude Gassho, note it in your calendar or planner.

Use the same procedure as described for the Harmony Gassho except that your recitation is the word "gratitude." The underlying sentiment accompanying the Gratitude Gassho is an awareness of interdependency—that you are supported by nature, by other people, by everything. There is a feeling of "counting your blessings," of "grace," or "how grateful I am." The seed of this sentiment will naturally blossom and be expressed in compassionate ways.

Everyday Gassho

Putting your hands together in Gassho can be broadened to include different creative hand gestures that can be related to a variety of themes or everyday activities. You are encouraged to discover or create your own Gasshos.

The Bright Dawn Center of Oneness Buddhism publishes a quarterly newsletter, *Oneness*, and in each publication, there is a column called "YES: Your Everyday Spirituality." The column is formatted for the three months of the current season, describing a creative Gassho to use as practice for each month.

In the current issue the Gassho for October is "Falling Leaf Gassho" and the theme is "Autumn Maple Leaf." The purpose is "Living a Natural Life" and the method is: "Start with a one-handed Gassho, then slowly twist your wrist back and forth as you lower your hand to waist level. Liken this movement to how an Autumn Maple leaf falls, showing front, showing back. Try to live such a natural life, without artificiality or pretensions!"

Important Considerations

You may already be familiar with Gassho and perhaps you're wondering why it is such a big deal. You may even think that Gassho is something simplistic and perhaps narrow in scope and effect. However, the Harmony and Gratitude Gassho as previously described are only a beginning. They are two handy tools for your spiritual tool bag. There are many more tools or different kinds of Gassho that can be added to your spiritual tool bag.

As you add tools such as Gassho, your spiritual path will become deeper and richer as your awareness of the many ways we act without thinking—without intention—and how adding intention to even simple everyday practices like Gassho can make it a profound spiritual practice that deepens your understanding of Buddhist teachings and heightens your appreciation and awareness of life and the people around you.

Many people need to be liberated from the idea of spiritual practice as only being practices authorized and approved by some authority. There is definitely a place for the time-tested traditional rituals handed down through a particular lineage. These rituals need not be rejected. It is not a matter of advocating that something is taken away but rather of adding something.

Modern spirituality requires flexibility of attitude in order to internalize and make the ancient truths relevant to each of us. Spirituality is individual and personal. Individual creativity in spiritual practice does not have to be viewed as an egotistic act that threatens established ways of doing things. You can give yourself permission to express yourself and be creative in the application of traditional or established practices. Growth means being open to change, both for individuals and institutions. If a particular traditional way works for someone and nothing else is desired, this is fine too. It is not necessarily an either/or situation when it comes to your personal spiritual path. Do what works for you and don't judge others who are doing things in other ways.

Being non-judgmental is of great value in living life with inner peace and in harmony with others. Diversity in spiritual paths is okay. You may start out in a narrow, sectarian tradition and by following this path in-depth, your spirituality may mature and come to be expressed in very open, liberal ways. Conversely, you may start out exploring many different individualized spiritual paths and, as a result, come to settle on one particular way as the best for you.

All paths have value because what is of value depends on time, place, and person. The word value is being used here not with regard to religious truth or teachings themselves but rather how you access, apply, or express such truth or teachings. It is important to examine the assumptions you might have about the nature of spirituality and spiritual practice. Such examination is especially helpful when you feel you aren't making progress spiritually. When spiritual growth does take place, your assumptions about the whole process often undergoes change too.

Whatever spiritual path you are on, keep a "beginner's mind." Don't get overly attached to your answers and conclusions. At the same time, remember that no matter what happens, nothing is wasted. All your experiences have their place in your spiritual journey. Enjoy the journey itself; the journey is not just a means to get to a destination. Don't ever think you have arrived. Keep going, keep going. Just be sincere, and don't forget to laugh.

Reflection on Right Intention

Full Bloom – Lilac

Each year you create yourself
out of gnarled gray wood—
flashes of purple on first green—
your sweet essence rises
after the dew and barely lingers
until evening breezes incite
my awareness of you.

Some years I barely notice
the sensation you are—
trapped inside my gray brain—
nurturing the black and white
of each scentless thought
in some misguided belief
that I am the miracle.

~Wendy Shinyo Haylett

Right Speech Practice: When to Speak; When to Listen

For the Right Speech practice tip, I suggest trying something inspired by what I've observed in myself and in those around me. As I've talked about in earlier sections, a combination of conditions that include social media and cable news, have created an openly divisive culture where we separate ourselves with political, religious, racial, sex, sexual preference, and economic labels that create "others" out of anyone who doesn't think like, look like, or believe like us.

Once those labels and boxes have divided us, we stop listening to each other. We believe we know that our side is right and everyone else is the "other" so they have nothing to say that we would want to hear. We get on social media and talk at each other rather than with each other, and we stop having dialogue with people who don't believe what we believe.

This environment that surrounds us supports reaction rather than wise action and reactive speaking rather than listening. How do we change the environment? As is the case with everything we've discussed up to this point, we first need to change ourselves. In the case of learning to listen, it starts with observing your behavior and your thoughts while in a conversation.

You can practice this by purposely focusing on a conversation with someone. You can choose someone you share the same views with first, then expand your practice to a conversation with someone who doesn't share your views. While in conversation notice when you have an urge to speak. Many times you will be speaking before you noticed that you had the urge to speak. That is reactive speaking. And reactive speaking tends to fill up the space where your conversation partner would feel invited to speak by your silence, by your active listening.

You will likely notice this reactive speaking habit to be more automatic and frequent when conversing with someone who doesn't share your views rather than the person who does. Yet, even when conversing with a person you are very comfortable with, you still might discover yourself jumping in to speak without stopping to notice if you thought about it first.

This is the practice. Be mindful of your urge to speak and ask yourself if what you are about to say adds to the conversation and is helpful. In other words, ask yourself if what you want to say is truthful, peaceful, gentle, and meaningful or if it's reactive.

Reflection on Right Speech

Many Colors of Water

Thinking of words I never spoke, I turn away from the path, stoop to hear a rock. It is much louder than the clamor of concealed expression—louder than its own polished image. Rocks talk in words not yet formed, singing the poetry of everything. Primordial language speaks what is without parenthetical distractions—how leaves are blue, the many colors of water, boundless emotion. I know you understand the dialect—it rushes from you in dreams while not in your own body, or as some spirit watcher. At morning, you surface from the flood of words knowing what you sound like, but not able to pronounce you again. Our stories live in these silent stanzas—I will let the rocks narrate me until you can hear without words.

~ Wendy Shinyo Haylett

Right Action Practice: Vow Tracking & The Pause

I recommend keeping a journal to track your thoughts, speech, and actions. This was a practice given by one of my teachers, originating from a practice done by Tibetan monks. The monks would go through the day and for each negative deed they committed, they would put a black stone in one pocket, and for each positive action, they would put a white stone in the other pocket. At the end of the day, they reviewed their stone totals and reflected on how they could do better.

You can do the same thing with a notebook or smartphone, checking yourself every two, three, or four hours. Pick one of the Freedom Vows to track all day. You note what you were thinking, saying, or doing in the last two- or four-hour period, before you've forgotten. You will be surprised at what you discover about yourself.

Not only does this practice build mindfulness into your day, but it is also very effective in correcting mindless habits that you wish you didn't have. If you commit to this practice for a long enough time you will notice a trend. You might notice that you repeat similar negative thoughts, speech, or actions throughout the day and from day-to-day. Don't be discouraged. Now that you are aware of it, you will form an intention to correct those actions.

This is where the pause comes in. You now know that you tend to repeat this behavior and you have the intention to stop it. That is all your mind needs to be watchful. Being alert helps you to observe what thoughts or feelings come before the behavior you're trying to curb. Then, the next time you notice the warning sign, you can pause.

Reflections on Right Action

Practice of the Path

Walking this path for years
I don't see it snaking
subtle left, wrap right
into wild.

I don't look for the perfect way,
never thought where
just walk—
practice of the path.

No self directing,
my stride continues on its own
until the scrub of white ash—
a gentle shoot bows to the sky.

Turning from the bounds
of walking, walker, destination,
being the path—
The path arrives at me.

~ Wendy Shinyo Haylett

Right Livelihood Practice: Five Daily Guidelines

As I wrote about in the previous reflection, right livelihood is deeper and broader than just work. It is right living. Living with an understanding of how everything you do touches every being in the world. The practice of Five Daily Life Guidelines offered by The Bright Dawn Center of Oneness Buddhism will help transform simple daily habits into right living. By using this practice to observe and guide your thoughts and behavior—in your work and when you're not working—you will be practicing right living. I offer deep bows of gratitude to Rev. Koyo Kubose for this practice and for letting me share it in this book.

Five Daily Life Guidelines:

- **CONSUME MINDFULLY:** Eat sensibly and don't be wasteful. Pause before buying; see if breathing is enough. Pay attention to the effects of media consumed.

- **SHARE LOVING-KINDNESS:** Consider other people's views deeply. Work for peace at every level. Spread joy, not negativity.

- **PRACTICE GRATITUDE:** Respect the people encountered; they are our teachers. Be equally grateful for opportunities and challenges. Notice where help is needed and be quick to act.

- **DISCOVER WISDOM:** Find connections between teachings and daily life. Do not become attached to conclusions. Mute the judgmental tongue.

- **ACCEPT CONSTANT CHANGE:** Be open to whatever arises in every moment. Cultivate "Beginner's Mind." Keep going, keep going.

Note: You can find the above on the central website of Bright Dawn: http://www.brightdawn.org/. Then click on the tab, "Spiritual Resources" where you will find a drop-down menu, "Daily Dharma."

Reflection on Right Livelihood

Spirit of Place

Our neighbors on this earth: woods, rivers, and fields always welcome us to their magnificent homes. Coming from neighborhoods where streams are paved, our anxious steps are slowed, disciplined by stalks, rocks, and stems, forcing our attention to earth, sky, and branches bowing to meet us. The ground, littered with shed feathers, the stirring of long-legged spiders, and wooly bears on the move; the sky, a goldfinch drills a stem for seed, chickadees swoop, and chattering sparrows dart from tree to tree—we don't understand what they're saying, but we know it's the source of our strength. The spirits of the land aren't lost, they're just waiting for people to hang around long enough to know them. Seeing, hearing and knowing what others can't or won't say—a bed of moss, crickets scampering, grasses whitened by harsh frost, bees gliding—a transformative power hidden in your attention to their gracious and magical universe, where the stains of an artificial environment are washed by a spirit of place that recognizes itself.

~ Wendy Shinyo Haylett

Right Effort Practice: Adjust Your Habits

Typically, things aren't as hard as we imagine them to be. That's what "right" effort is all about. It's enough. Not too much; not too little. Just right. Right view plus intention and attention are all you need. What follows is a suggestion on how to apply right effort as an easy practice you can take up with "joyous effort."

Maybe list two or three things that you do—and wish you didn't or have regrets about doing—that you could try harder not to do and/or two or three things that you could try to incorporate in your life to make yourself and those around you happier.

It's about paying attention. It's about noticing. This is, in essence, right effort. This is the hard part. Adjusting your habits after noticing them isn't nearly as tough. Ask yourself where do you make too much effort or not enough? Where are you lazy or running on habit? Where are you too externally focused? Or too internally focused? It's about looking at yourself, the people and world outside of your head and noticing. Really notice. Pause your head stories and notice what's going on around you. Notice what you are doing.

Our habits have a powerful hold on us. We sleep-walk through our days with our habits in the lead. But once we try reducing or eliminating one bad habit or adding one good one and it works, it's empowering!

As an example, I will share my practice. First, I will list two things I will try to slowly eliminate, followed by two things I will try to do more of. Then it's your turn!

Two things I'm going to try to eliminate:

- Impatience with my family (spouse and dog) when I'm under time pressure or frustrations of feeling inadequate and unprepared. You will notice here that I've already taken the first big step of knowing my triggers: time constraints and frustrating feelings.

- Making quick judging comments about others, either silently or shared with others.

Two things I'm going to try to incorporate:

- When I feel driven or feel the tug of perfectionism, I will try to purposely take a walk around the yard or do a 10-minute meditation.

- I will try to always be conscious of listening more than speaking and try not to interrupt.

Reflection on Right Effort

Narrow Passage

Sometimes I struggle—twist and turn—
aiming at the narrow gap of me.
Drifting from shadows of steep conformity
a light appears, blazes through my brain,
engulfs my heart and uncovers my original self...

a vast conflicting wilderness of everything—
bad and good, stagnant brown and flowing blue,
desire and contentment,
choking grasses and a brilliant flame of maple leaves,
heaven and hell—

and nothing...

Life without force, not even emptiness
to steer for.

~ Wendy Shinyo Haylett

Right Mindfulness Practice: Unified Mindfulness

I referred to the Unified Mindfulness approach to meditation earlier in this chapter. **This system of meditation helps strengthen your concentration power, sensory clarity, and equanimity.**

Concentration power is the ability of selective attention.

Sensory clarity is the ability to clearly distinguish visual, auditory, and bodily sensations from each other, separating the threads of experience. It is also the ability to note when a sensory event arises and note when it passes.

Equanimity is the ability to remain calm and non-reactive despite the situation or experience. It is strengthened by the wisdom of knowing nothing is permanent in life and things come and they go. Despite it sometimes being considered as aloofness or coolness, it is much more of a warm acceptance of life. It is the ability to overcome the instinct to grasp and cling.

The Unified Mindfulness meditation system strengthens these three powers through a method of meditation that can best be described as a unification of *samatha* or calm abiding and *vipassana* or insight meditation. The method is built on a See-Hear-Feel practice.

See-Hear-Feel Practice is the noticing where your attention is focused based on three sensory categories.

- See includes what you see in your environment and also what you see in your imagination.

- Hear includes what you hear in your environment and also what you hear in your mind, like talking to yourself or hearing a tune stuck in your head.

- Feel includes physical sensations and emotional feelings.

A quick introduction to the practice is to notice where your attention goes from moment to moment. Keep your attention on what you notice for a few seconds then move to the next experience you notice. Decide whether what you're noticing is "see", "hear", or "feel." If you're not sure what category, go ahead and guess. If you notice more than one, just pick one to focus on. And if you notice too many at once and miss labeling some, that's fine, too.

Once you identify the category, label it by saying out loud or to yourself, "see" or "hear" or "feel". If you notice the same experience twice, it's fine to repeat the label. Keep a steady pace and even tone when you label what you're noticing.

The key to this practice is that it's easy to do, it works with what's around you at any moment, and you can do the practice at any time. When you engage in this practice, you will find your concentration and sensory clarity does improve rapidly. And if practice long enough you will notice the feeling of equanimity.

This is just an introduction. To discover more about this practice, you can take their free core training, which you can find out more about here: https://unifiedmindfulness.com/core.

Reflection on Right Mindfulness & Concentration

The Purelands

Somewhere beyond the fence,
or before,
a vast space that can't be contained by fences
arises
in a glimpse
of your own light—

lacking nothing
being everything:
rotted wood, a crystalline sky,
bent nails, a field mouse, jeweled grasses
and the hoax of self—

reflected perfectly
in your heart mind—
mirror of infinite light
radiant and perfect—
from the spaciousness
between your thoughts.

~ Wendy Shinyo Haylett

PART FIVE: THE LIST OF LISTS

THE LIST OF LISTS

The Four Noble Truths

The Four Noble Truths for Everyday Buddhism:

- **Awareness: Life is crappy sometimes and we suffer.** This is the Awareness and understanding we need to get familiar with and know to be the truth of our human existence. Awareness prevents fear and confusion. Awareness is the first principle of the Buddha's teaching because it is necessary to first be aware of how things really are before we can begin to accept, appreciate, and act in the ways we must act to minimize our own and others' suffering.

- **Acceptance: We suffer not necessarily because life is crappy.** I'm sure we've all had the experience of being relatively content EVEN when we are in a shitty phase of life. We don't suffer because of the circumstance in our lives but because we grasp or cling to things being something other than they are. We grasp at things we want and don't have; we grasp at getting rid of the stuff we don't want. The way to ease or eliminate that suffering is to learn to adopt an attitude of active Acceptance. As my Sensei and his father, Gyomay Kubose, taught: "Acceptance IS transcendence."

- **Appreciation: There is a way out.** The way out offers a path of sincere appreciation for the teachings of the Buddha and the new awareness and acceptance that we now have for life as it is. This is the Appreciation phase. When we stop

269

focusing on things we want but don't have or pushing away things we have but don't want, the things that are right in front of us take on a new shine. We truly begin to experience life. We appreciate everything in our life.

- **Action: The way out is practicing the Eightfold Path. This is the Action Path.** When we are aware of things as they are and we begin to accept and appreciate life as we experience it, the right actions become more obvious and sensible to us. "Right" actions are the way the actions of The Eightfold Path are phrased, as the right actions to take. Yet we need to chill a bit around the rightness of right. These are not commandments or moral directives but suggestions about what actions may be the most effective. When studying and practicing the Eightfold Path, relaxing your grip on the necessity or "rightness" of having to do certain things exactly the way you interpret this "rightness" will be beneficial for you. Think of the word "right" in this respect as the suggestions your trainer, Yoga teacher, piano teacher, or golf pro might give you to help your practice.

The Four Noble Truths are traditionally expressed:

- **The unenlightened life is "suffering.** That life is suffering is the "bad news of Buddhism." Yet, a better translation of the "dukkha" or suffering is "difficult" or unsatisfactory."

- **The cause of this suffering is craving, or attachment or grasping.** When you like something you want to grab it, possess it, keep it FOREVER. This stems from ignorance about the nature of reality—the nature of what it is that really makes you happy.

- **The cessation of dukkha, or suffering, is possible**, and the end is liberation or the realization of nirvana or enlightenment (bliss and inner freedom).

- **The path or way to the end of suffering is explained through the teaching of the Eightfold Path**, which is the practice to achieve happiness for yourself and others—and, eventually, enlightenment.

The Eightfold Path

1. Right View

2. Right Intention

3. Right Speech

4. Right Action

5. Right Livelihood

6. Right Effort

7. Right Mindfulness

8. Right Concentration

The Three Sufferings

- **The suffering of suffering.** This is the obvious suffering—what most people equate with suffering—actual physical or emotional pain. Illness, injury, loss, grief or even disappointment.

- **The suffering of change.** This is the fact that your body, mind, and all the people and circumstances of your life constantly change and deteriorate. This is what one of my teachers used to summarize as, "attached to every pleasant experience is a lousy end." Whether it's the last of the cookies, or the death of a pet or family member, or the loss of a job, it's all made of the stuff that will change, decline, or disappear.

- **The suffering of conditioned existence, or pervasive suffering.** This is the suffering that results from having a condition, or nature, that is impermanent and changeable, based on the conditions that bring our bodies, minds, all phenomena, and all circumstances into existence. It is this conditioned existence that causes the process of aging and dying, which begins at the moment of conception. It's the nature of our existence.

The Four Thoughts That Turn the Mind to Dharma

- **Precious human existence:** This precious human birth, which is favorable for practicing the Dharma, is hard to obtain and easily lost, so I must make it meaningful.

- **Death, mortality, and impermanence:** The world and all its inhabitants are impermanent. The life of each being is like a water bubble. It is uncertain when I will die, and only Dharma can help me live and die more peacefully, so I must practice now with diligence.

- **The Law of Karma:** Because I create my own karma, I should abandon all unwholesome action. Keeping this in mind, I must observe my mind each day.

- **The problems of our normal conditioned existence:** Like a feast before the executioner leads me to my death, the homes, friends, pleasures, and possessions of this life cause me continual torment by means of the three sufferings (introduced before in the Basic Buddhist Teachings section). I must cut through all attachment and strive to attain right view and eventual enlightenment, or inner peace.

The Three Kinds of Right Intention

- The intention of **renunciation**, which counters the intention of desire.

- The intention of **goodwill**, which counters the intention of ill will.

- The intention of **harmlessness**, which counters the intention of harmfulness.

The Four Restraints in Right Speech

- Refrain from lying; practice **truthful** speech;

- Refrain from divisive talk; practice **peaceful** speech;

- Refrain from harsh words; practice **gentle** speech;

- Refrain from idle talk; practice **meaningful** speech.

The Five Precepts

The "Everyday Buddhism" Approach to the Five Precepts:

- I will **protect and support life** and strive to love and understand others.

- I will **take only what is freely given** and practice gratitude and generosity.

- I will **respect and support on-going relationships**, honor my commitments, and practice discernment in sexual activity without compulsiveness.

- I will **say what is true, useful, and timely,** and practice deep listening so that my speaking and listening reflect loving-kindness and compassion.

- I will **maintain a clear and alert mind** that is aware of its motivations, moment-to-moment so that I can discern between what is the cause of suffering and what is not the cause of suffering.

The typical presentation of the Five Precepts is in a negative or restraint presentation:

- **Do not kill** (refrain from destroying living creatures).

- **Do not steal** (refrain from taking what is not given).

- **Do not misuse sex** (refrain from sexual misconduct).

- **Do not lie** (refrain from incorrect speech).

- **Do not indulge in intoxicants** (refrain from substances leading to carelessness).

The Freedom Vows

Of the body:

- **Nourish life.** Do things to protect life. Did you move a pencil off the stairway that someone might have slipped on? You're not going to get a chance to throw someone out of the way of a speeding taxi or invent a vaccine every day. Did you give aspirin to someone at work? Did you make tea for someone with a sniffle? This is protecting life.

- **Honor people's property.** Did you take the last of the toilet paper from the bathroom and make sure it was replaced for the next person? Did you pick up that tiny piece of Kleenex that just fell out of your purse and put it in your pocket or purse to throw away later, or did you leave it on the floor? Stuff that small matters. Heaven is built on small things. An empty bucket can be filled by drops of water. You don't have to be Mother Teresa to have an impact on others' happiness.

- **Are you sexually pure (not necessarily celibate, but pure?) and are you faithful in your relationships with others?** If you are engaging in sex, are you obsessed about it or thinking about it all day, or doing it in improper places at improper times, and with improper people? A healthy sexual, normal, relationship is fine. Adultery, of course, is not. Does it bother your peace of mind? That's the question. Are you maintaining the level of sexual purity that you've committed to? For a married person it would be, did you check out someone else's partner today? Just for a second, did you think that way? Don't let it obsess your life. Honor your own and other people's commitments and don't ever cross that line.

Of the speech:

- **Be truthful**. Try to be totally truthful all day long. Are you required to tell someone how bad their dress looks if they ask you for your opinion? Change the subject. Drop your pencil or coffee cup. If it would hurt the person in some way, or make them very angry, or if it's very destructive, it's best to slide out of it, if you can. The key, again, is your intention. Would it hurt the other person or would it help them?

- **Do you speak in ways that bring people together?** Do you, in your everyday conversations, try to bring people close together? Once in a while, you meet a person who's really good at this. I have a friend who will run up to you and say, "I've got someone you have to meet! You'll love this person!" He introduces you and you become best friends. Do you see what I mean? Because our normal human tendency is, "Did you hear what he said about you?" Our tendency is to do the opposite. Find ways to bring people together with your words.

- **Speak gently.** Gentle, thoughtful. Don't talk trash talk at work to "be one of the guys" and expect to have a habit of gentle speech during the other hours. And don't talk in sweet ways when you're not feeling sweet at all. Like when you say, "Have a nice day," but what you really mean is "Go to hell." Your speech is judged by your intent. Speak gently and think gently.

- **Speak meaningfully.** Whenever you open your mouth, try to say something that has some kind of relevance to the person's life. Don't yap about the horrible thing a political or entertainment personality did. Or about stuff that doesn't matter, stuff that doesn't help anybody. Don't complain about people or things in the news or just waste talk, okay? Before you open your mouth, ask yourself if you're about to say something meaningful.

Of the mind:

- **When you see someone else achieve something or get something, be happy for them.** What's the opposite of that? It's like jealousy or unhappiness when somebody gets something nice. When something good happens to somebody else, you rush up and say, "I'm so happy you got that promotion! You really deserve it." Try to consciously experience the joy in other people's successes. Our human tendency is to be jealous. As budding bodhisattvas, we are committed to the goal of bringing every happiness to every sentient being. So, don't think, "I don't see why he got the promotion!"

- **Try to really feel for people suffering misfortune, no matter how famous they are or how much you don't like them.** When someone is suffering in some way, take the time and the effort to try to empathize with them. The normal human tendency is to do the opposite. "Oh, so-and-so got caught in bank fraud or a sexual scandal! His life is ruined! Tell me more!" There's this human tendency to be fascinated by other people's problems, especially famous people's problems.

"So and so committed suicide? Why? How?" This is the big thing in social media and on cable TV. People seem to love to hear about the misfortune of others. You need to think the opposite way. When you hear about something like that, your thought should be, "Oh, I'm sorry for his family, and I feel really bad about it and I wish that wouldn't happen to anyone." It's the opposite of being fascinated by other people's problems. You truly try to put yourself in their place. Try to have extensive empathy or compassion for other people's problems, rather than this secret little joy about them. It's a weird human tendency. You're not upset by it, you are fascinated by it.

- **Maintain a Buddhist worldview.** Understand that all good things come from helping other people and bad things come from looking out for your own interests, only. You can watch out for your own interests, but equally, watch out for other people's interests.

The Five Daily Guidelines

- **CONSUME MINDFULLY:** Eat sensibly and don't be wasteful. Pause before buying; see if breathing is enough. Pay attention to the effects of media consumed.

- **SHARE LOVING-KINDNESS:** Consider other people's views deeply. Work for peace at every level. Spread joy, not negativity.

- **PRACTICE GRATITUDE:** Respect the people encountered; they are our teachers. Be equally grateful for opportunities and challenges. Notice where help is needed and be quick to act.

- **DISCOVER WISDOM:** Find connections between teachings and daily life. Do not become attached to conclusions. Mute the judgmental tongue.

- **ACCEPT CONSTANT CHANGE:** Be open to whatever arises in every moment. Cultivate "Beginner's Mind." Keep going, keep going.

The Four Aspects of Right Effort

- The effort to prevent unwholesome qualities, especially greed, anger, and ignorance, from arising.

- The effort to extinguish unwholesome qualities that have already arisen.

- The effort to cultivate skillful, or wholesome, qualities, especially generosity, loving-kindness, and wisdom (the opposites of greed, anger, and ignorance) that have not yet arisen.

- The effort to strengthen the wholesome qualities that have already arisen.

The Five Hindrances: Try Not to Do

- Sensual desire

- Ill will

- Dullness and drowsiness

- Restlessness and worry

- Doubt

The Three Types of Destructive Thinking

- Thinking covetously

- Thinking with malice

- Thinking with antagonism

The Four Foundations of Mindfulness

- Mindfulness of the Body

- Mindfulness of Feelings

- Mindfulness of Mind

- Mindfulness of Mind Objects

The Five Hindrances to Meditation

- Desire

- Aversion

- Sloth

- Restlessness

- Doubt

ABOUT THE AUTHOR

WENDY SHINYO HAYLETT is a Buddhist teacher and lay minister with The Bright Dawn Center of Oneness Buddhism. She is the host of the podcast, *Everyday Buddhism: Making Everyday Better*, and also works as a behavioral and communication coach, career and life coach, meditation teacher, and spiritual companion.

Wendy has 25+ years of coaching experience, helping people live their lives and navigate their careers with more mindfulness and resilience. She lives in Fairport, New York with her spouse, Renée Seiyo Phillips and their dog, Bella. Renée is an artist, illustrator, and also a lay minister with The Bright Dawn Center of Oneness Buddhism.

ACKNOWLEDGMENTS

INTERDEPENDENCE IS A FOUNDATIONAL PRINCIPLE IN BUDDHISM. The publishing of this book could not have happened without a very long list of people who have helped in big and small ways.

First to my spouse, partner, and teacher, Renée Seiyo Phillips, who put up with my being unavailable many times, as I devoted the last 10 months to the planning and writing of this book. My mind was preoccupied almost constantly, which left little mental space for engaged conversations, patience, and play. I apologize for being so out of touch much of the time and promise to be more present.

To my treasured friend, author who has gone before, motivator, and editor, Julie Scipioni McKown. Without you, this book would have remained a dream. Thank you for showing me the way to make it real, ensuring I stayed on task, and being an awesome editor and more awesome friend.

A sincere bow to my niece, Laura Nespoli, for her keen insight into marketing and branding strategy that helped clarify my vision for cover design and promotional messaging.

Without my Sensei, Rev. Koyo Kubose, there would be no Everyday Buddhism podcast and no book. And that's just a tiny piece of what you've brought to my life. Without you, I would have never understood the everyday that is Buddhism and the Buddhism that is everyday. Thank you, too, for letting me share the gentle wisdom of Bright Dawn's teaching.

Bows to my good friends Christopher Kakuyo Ross-Leibow and Michael Shinyo Lawrence who continue to give me emotional and spiritual support and challenging Buddhist topics to think about. Thanks also to Noah Mayo Rasheta for inspiration, and all my Bright Dawn Family for being sangha and teachers for me.

Special thanks to the members of the Everyday Sangha, my sangha, teachers, and friends, who helped me sample the content of this book in our meetings. And a HUGE thank you to all the Everyday Buddhism podcast listeners everywhere. You are the ones that lit the fire of inspiration for this book.

PERMISSIONS & REFERENCES

Stephen Batchelor, *Secular Buddhism: Imagining the Dharma in an Uncertain World.* (New Haven & London: Yale University Press, 2017). Page 11, 14, 15.

Shantideva, *The Way of the Bodhisattva*, translated by the Padmakara Translation Group, © 1997, 2006 by the Padmakara Translation Group. Reprinted by arrangement with The Permissions Company, LLC on behalf of Shambala Publications Inc., Boulder, CO. www.shambhala.com. Pages 16, 24.

David Brazier, *The Feeling Buddha: A Buddhist Psychology of Character*, Adversity and Passion (New York: Fromm International, 2000). Pages 42, 156.

Gregg Krech, *The Art of Taking Action: Lessons from Japanese Psychology* (Monkton, Vermont: ToDo Institute, 2014). Page 72.

Miguel Angel Ruiz, M.D. and Janet Mills, *The Four Agreements*, © 1997. (Produced with permission of Amber-Allen Publishing, Inc., P.O. Box 6657, San Rafael, California 94903. All rights reserved). Page 89.

Geshe Kelsang Gyatso, *Meaningful to Behold: The Bodhisattva's Way of Life* (Sonoma, California: Unfettered Mind Media, 2016). Pages 154, 162.

Thubten Chodron, from a series of teachings based on the "The Gradual Path to Enlightenment" (Lamrim). https://thubtenchodron.org/1994/07/generate-effort-wisdom/. Page 175.

Ken McLeod, *A Trackless Path*. A commentary on the great completion (Dzogchen) teaching of Jigmé Lingpas's "Revelations of Ever-present Good." (London: Tharpa Publications, 1994). Page 198.

Unified Mindfulness, https://unifiedmindfulness.com/. Page 228, 229.

REQUEST FOR REVIEW

IF YOU ENJOYED THIS BOOK AND FOUND IT USEFUL, I WOULD BE VERY GRATEFUL IF YOU POSTED AN HONEST REVIEW. Your support matters and really does make a difference. Think of it as a practice in Right Speech and Right Action. :)

If you'd like to leave a review, go to the review section on the book's Amazon page. You will see this:

Review this product

Share your thoughts with other customers

> Write a customer review

Just click on the link and write your review. Thanks again for your support.

Please share your thoughts about what you learned from this book with your friends and family. And check out the podcast for more Everyday Buddhism: http://everyday-buddhism.libsyn.com/

MORE EVERYDAY BUDDHISM

THERE IS SO MUCH MORE FOR YOU TO EXPLORE …

In the podcast, Everyday Buddhism: Making Everyday Better:

http://everyday-buddhism.libsyn.com/

At the Everyday Buddhism website:

https://www.everyday-buddhism.com/

At the Everyday Buddhism Public Facebook group:

https://www.facebook.com/groups/308497089951447/

Or join the Everyday Buddhism Sangha:

donorbox.org/supporters-bonus-content-membership

6125593535R00166